Epochal Reckonings

J. P. Linstroth

Proverse Hong Kong

2020

Cover photo: Hurrican Katrina in the Gulf of Mexico
by NASA Visible Earth
https://upload.wikimedia.org/ ᵃⁿᵉ/a/a4/Hurric
ane_Katrina_August_28_200

D1059859

Proverse Hong Kong full istic
expression. The views and oject
are those of the author alone and do not repr nd of
Proverse Hong Kong or that of any other person named in this
text.

*Care has been taken to respect the rights of all. If there has
been any omission, remedy will be made in a revised edition in
due course if information is received.*

In *Epochal Reckonings,* poet, adjunct professor and editorial writer, J.P. Linstroth describes and responds to some of the crises of the first years of the 21st century. He aims, as he puts it, to cause concern, discussion, and surprise, as well as to evoke the emotions of anger, empathy, and sadness. The events covered include the huge migrations of people seeking to cross borders, whether in the Americas, Asia, Africa, the Middle-East or Europe, hoping for safety and a better life. Linstroth also shows and comments on human and natural acts of astonishing violence: the 9/11 destruction of the twin towers of the World Trade Center in New York; the Hurricane named Katrina of 2005; the Haitian earthquake of 2010. Linstroth portrays man's inhumanity to man, whether callous, careless, mistaken, or deliberate: the police-killings of African-American youths; the genocide of Brazilian indigenous peoples; the torture of Iraqi prisoners at Abu Ghraib prison; mass school-shootings in the USA; and the Yemeni civil war. Linstroth describes his poetry as emergent and inchoate, outlining the struggles and sufferings of various groups during major crises in the 21st century, embodied by racism, extremism, violence, and tragedies too many to be told. These poems capture such calamities, defining their symbolic significance for many of those who have experienced these disasters of our times across the globe.

J. P. Linstroth lives in the United States and has been writing poetry since he was a boy. He obtained a D.Phil. (PhD) in Social and Cultural Anthropology from the University of Oxford and is an Adjunct Professor at Barry University and Faculty Member at the Catholic University of New Spain (UCNE). His books include: *Marching Against Gender Practice: Political Imaginings in the Basqueland* (2015, Lexington Books) and: *The Forgotten Shore* (Poetic Matrix Press, 2017). Linstroth was a signatory of the Brussels Declaration for Peace to end ETA violence (2010). He was a co-recipient of an Alexander von Humboldt Foundation Grant (2005-2007) to study immigrant populations: Cubans, Haitians, and Guatemalan-Mayan immigrants in South Florida. He was awarded a J. William Fulbright Foreign Scholar Grant (2008-2009) to study urban Amerindians in Manaus, Brazil and to be a Visiting Professor at the Universida de Federal do Amazonas (UFAM). In 2017, he was awarded a Presidential Lifetime Achievement Award. Linstroth is a member of the Board of Directors of the International Peace Research Association Foundation (IPRAF). In 2019, he received a medal as a "Gentleman of Merit" and was inducted into *La Noble Compañia de Bernardo de Galvez* (The Noble Order of Bernardo de Galvez). In addition to many academic articles, he writes "opinion editorials" ("Op-Eds") in many newspapers and online news sources, including *CounterPunch, Des Moine Register, Euroscientist, L.A. Progressive, PeaceVoice, The Houston Chronicle,* and *Londonderry Sentinel.* His academic research interests are cognition, ethno-nationalism, gender, genocide, history, immigrant advocacy, indigeneity, indigenous politics, indigenous rights, love, memory, minority rights, peace, peace-building, racism, social justice, and trauma.

2 Epochal Reckonings

Epochal Reckonings

J. P. Linstroth

Winner of the Proverse Prize 2019

Proverse Hong Kong

Epochal Reckonings
By J.P. Linstroth
First edition published in paperback in Hong Kong
by Proverse Hong Kong, under sole and exclusive licence,
November 2020.
ISBN 13: 978-988-8491-94-0

Copyright © J.P. Linstroth

Enquiries to Proverse Hong Kong
P.O. Box 259, Tung Chung Post Office,
Lantau, NT, Hong Kong SAR, China.
Email: proverse@netvigator.com;
Web: www.proversepublishing.com

Cover photo by NASA Visible Earth
Author photo by Elsy Aumann
Cover design by Artist Hong Kong.

British Library Cataloguing in Publication Data
A catalogue record for the first paperback edition
is available from the British Library

PRIOR PUBLICATION ACKNOWLEDGEMENTS

I acknowledge, with thanks, kind permission to include the following poems, first published as shown below.
'El Norte' in *Constellations: A Journal of Poetry and Fiction*, Vol. 8, (2018) pp. 56-57.
'The Crossing' in *Mingled Voices*, 3, the International Proverse Poetry Prize Anthology, 2018 (2019), pp. 92-93;
'Eco por Un Grito Moderno' in J.P. Linstroth, "Border Policies from Hell", opinion-editorial, in *CounterPunch*, (June 28, 2019, https://www.counterpunch.org/2019/06/28/border-policies-from-hell/)/

DEDICATION

This book is dedicated to my mother, Dr. Carol Ann Dorgan.
I am eternally grateful for her unconditional love and
her continual belief in me and all of my endeavours.

Likewise, this book is dedicated to all of the "victims" of "epochal
reckonings" we have to account for around the world in the early
21st century. Most of these so-called victims are nameless.
Even so, it is the aspiration of this book
to give all of these victims a voice
they may never have had otherwise.

ACKNOWLEDGEMENTS

Over the years, a person accumulates many personal debts, especially among family and friends. Without such a support network of people, writing a book such as this one would never be possible. Some more than others have greater importance, simply because they have greater significance in one's life. Among these are my mother Carol Dorgan, my father John P. Linstroth, Sr., my sister, Molly Del Re, and my brother, Michael Linstroth. So too, there are my brother-in-law, Joe Del Re, and my sister-in-law, Robyn Linstroth and my nieces, Ali and Peyton from my sister and brother-in-law, and my niece, Ruby, and nephew, Bo, from my brother and sister-in-law. One can never thank family enough for the love one derives from them, and therefore, I am most grateful to my family for all that I am and the writer I have become because of my family.

I would like to recognize a few of my friends. Please also know, while I try to recognize everyone, I may have forgotten some, and if so, please forgive me in my forgetfulness.

First and foremost, I am grateful to Conor Nixon for suggesting I should write poetry about contemporary issues.

Then there are my college friends: Bob Nix, Joseph Rondinelli, David Butler, John Stankard, John Forsythe, and Jim Seeley. There are also Oxford friends, David Waters, Lorcan Kennan, Frank Humphreys, Shond Laha, and Jon Stark; some Basque friends: Oier San Martin and Abraham Albisu; and academic colleagues, Hamdesa Tuso, Marie Olson-Lounsbery, David Sutton, Julia Chaitin, Otto Von Feigenblatt, José Exequiel Basini Rodrigues, Raimundo Nonato da Silva, Sandra Ott, Roger Goodman, Marcus Banks, and Jeremy MacClancy; and former PhD students, Patrick Hiller, Jackie Font-Guzman, Michael Fonkem, and Yanira Aleman-

Torres; and some new friends, Cassia Araujo, Claudia Cardona, Tatiana Parra, Beth Kline, Tony Spaniol, and Marshall Teitelbaum. I am also grateful to photographer, Elsy Aumann, for her wonderful photographs of me for this book. So too, I am grateful to editor and poet, John Peterson, for publishing my first volume of poetry. Also, I am appreciative of Ian Trottier for including me monthly on his radio show, "Discussions of Truth" as the "Linstroth Report". Further, I am indebted to Tom Hastings, Editor, for publishing my opinions in *PeaceVoice* and to Joshua Frank, Managing Editor, and to Jeffrey St. Clair, Editor, for publishing my opinions in *CounterPunch*. Moreover, I would be remiss if I did not recognize two very important primary school teachers, namely, Ralph Greco and Bob Bayless for introducing me to English literature and the Classics. Importantly too, I would like to recognize Aimée Valdes, manager of Restaurant Casa Santiago, for her friendship. Also, I would like to acknowledge my cousin and renowned poet, Ann Townsend, who is a continuous inspiration through her feminine and graceful poetic voice.

As a teacher at Royal Palm Beach High School, I would like to recognize the administration, faculty, and students there.

And finally, I would like to acknowledge with my profoundest gratitude, Dr. Gillian Bickley and Dr. Verner Bickley, Founders and Publishers of Proverse Publications for their kind support and bringing this volume to fruition. Additionally, I am immensely grateful to the Proverse Editorial Team for their careful editing of my poetry and formatting of this book.

And of course, to you too, the reader, for picking up and hopefully reading my work.

Thank you all with profound gratitude.

AUTHOR'S INTRODUCTION

In considering my present work, *Epochal Reckonings*, I had in mind a certain theme, which was to write about major events of concern in this new 21st century. What I wish the reader to have in mind when reading the following pages are some of the works by Michelangelo di Lodovico Buonarroti Simoni (1475-1564), the great architect, painter, and sculptor of the Italian Renaissance, simply known to most as "Michelangelo", but especially his works: *Prigioni* (Prisoners), or *Schiavi* (Slaves). These works were originally to adorn Pope Julius II's tomb but were "unfinished". Why should the reader think about Michelangelo and his *Prigioni* or *Schiavi* in relation to this book? To me, Michelangelo's sculptures may be symbolic of something other than what Michelangelo himself intended. I interpret them as symbolic of this book presented here, *Epochal Reckonings*. In this work, as Michelangelo's sculptured figures, the *Prigioni* or *Schiavi*, are caught in motion in marble, likewise my words here are meant to signify all of us as prisoners of this time and fettered to our epoch in this time. Thus, the following effort is a snapshot in time. And, as such, we are who we are because of the times we live in. Our time forms us and we are prisoners to this period in history, and perhaps, because we are humans, looking to be liberated beyond our times if possible. This book of poetry, *Epochal Reckonings*, may then be regarded as an "emergent text"; just as Michelangelo's *Prigioni* or *Schiavi* were sculpted from white marble, the black words are emergent on the white-pages herewith. These modest words presented here in a limited way form notions about the first years of the 21st century. Like Michelangelo's Carrara white marble figures, his prisoners struggling to be free, so are my words per se. Words within these white pages, like white marble, are carved into certain ideas and notions and inked about this age at the beginning of the 21st century and some of those issues which mark our age. The book itself is divided into nine differentiated parts with Greek and Latin subtitles for a total of 25 poems. These are: **Part I – Alpha** (Beginning), **Part II – Fines** (Borders), **Part III – Politikos** (Politicians), **Part IV – Terrere** (Frighten or Terrorize), **Part V – Natura** (Nature), **Part VI – Bellum** (War), **Part VII – Facticius** (Man-Made), **Part VIII – Mactans** (Slaughtering, Killing, Sacrificing), and **Part IX – Omega** (Ending). (Three of the poems herein, "The Crossing", "El Norte", and "Eco por Un Grito Moderno", were published elsewhere as recognized in the Acknowledgements.)

What is presented here then is optimistically an innovative collection of poetry and an attempt to capture the zeitgeist of these early years of the 21st century—marked mostly by tragedies. It is a book with the central theme of "racism", that is, racism against immigrants, migrants, and refugees; racism against African-Americans; racism against Iraqi prisoners of war; racism against Yemeni children; racism against Haitians; racism against Katrina victims; racism against Brazilian Amerindians and indigenous peoples everywhere; discrimination against homeless people; and overall a volume about minorities in general and their ongoing dilemmas and struggles. Herein are the silent voices and silenced voices of those, more often than not, unheard.

It is an incomplete work, or an emergent work, because no work of art can quite capture a period of time, or encapsulate an entire epoch in its entirety, but rather only sketch out some of its essences and its characteristics. Perhaps, others might see in this work something more akin to the *Venus de Milo*, as an imperfect expression of an artistic age, then ancient Greek sculpture, broken and incomplete from time, and here a fragmented and partial collection of poetry about a time. My words here, are thus incomplete, and are expressions of imperfection, and missing so much, but nonetheless, evocative of this time—the here and now. My words are feasibly inchoate and incipient, suggestive of this time, our here and now, yet, only excising some essential bits. I can only hope so and offer it to you the reader for your perusal.

More specifically, *Epochal Reckonings*, is conceived without pretention to summarize some of the great tragedies of our times: the Great Global Migration Crisis; the tragedy of 9/11; 2005

Hurricane Katrina; 2010 Haitian Earthquake; the last three U.S. presidential administrations (Bush, Obama, Trump); the genocide of Brazilian Amerindians; the torture of Iraqi prisoners at Abu Ghraib; the Yemeni Civil War; homelessness; the recent police killings of African-American young men; and the recent tragedies of school shootings in the United States. As such, this book, *Epochal Reckonings*, evokes the necessity of coming to a "reckoning", that is, coming to terms with and an accounting for these events. It is incomplete. Yet, it is emergent. It is engaging and yet the author through this writing is humbled from such tremendous human suffering.

In all, I hope the reader will find some solace in reading my words about these great tragedies of our times and perhaps even empathize with the human sufferings of our era from my mere words. But my words are only words. The words here in this volume cannot possibly expect to summarize all the traumas, all the losses, and all the humanity herein which they intend to symbolize. Yet, as any artist wishing their work has meaning, I too anticipate my words will aid the reader in visualizing these times in the early years of the 21st century. May the following words, if possible, evoke some emotions and some images for the reader, and convey their meanings. Perhaps, some of these words will be remembered too.

Thank you kindly for considering *Epochal Reckonings* and reading this book of poetry. May you find in it something evocative for you and something important to remember about our times.

J. P. Linstroth, D.Phil.
Palm Beach Gardens, Florida, USA
September 2019

12 Epochal Reckonings

EPOCHAL RECKONINGS

J.P. Linstroth

PART I

ALPHA

ALPHA

Coccineous scarlet frothings into bulbous obsidian mudlike
pourings forth
    Oozing violent into cobalt seas forming islands

New beginnings out of one great conical explosion of grey ash and
pumice
    In great fuliginous clouds cinereous clouds expanding into the
great azure

As the ocean swallows up coquelicot globs of bursting erupting soft
black rock
    Leaching out of the earth essence into gaseous waters boiling
and steaming

New ends devouring and consuming and engorging and ingesting
flora and fauna
    Palm trees burnt to cinder and scurrying lizards baked to
embers

As cardinal haematic cinnabar nacarat globs plop plop in heaps
upon restless indigo waters
    Transforming into piceous nigrine melanic ebony rocks

Heaping into rock upon rock upon rock upon rock
    Forming islands

18   Epochal Reckonings

PART II

FINES

THE CROSSING

Across stark ravines and arroyos
They crossed the Sonora
They were three plus their coyote

Organ pipe cacti stood tall in blue shadows
As if hidden men staring at them

They crossed

It was very, very dark except for a lantern moon
Its orb some enormous fish's eye in the great deep
Illuming depths of a fathomless ocean in the pitch blackness
Winking in and out of thin clouds crossing the dark skies

Along a worn sandy path, they encountered a woman and her child
They shared a cantina of tepid water
And if you could see their faces, you would see their desperation
But their faces were black in the shadows
And even in the cold desert night, they were sweating

Of a sudden there was a helicopter overhead
Irradiating the organ pipe cacti and the sage brush and the sand
And this great light searched them out

This light like a great illumined eye found them
As they were caught by the great beam

They began running in all directions, panicked and scared
Like lizards scurrying toward the shade of rocks in a beaming sun
And yet hiding from the raptor's eye of some maniacal mechanical
immense eagle

From a distance, headlights could be seen, coming toward them
Converging on them in three directions
Kicking up dust in the beams

Six shafts of light moving up and down
With the rusty dust wafting into the night air
As organ pipe cacti and sage brush illumed
Throwing haphazard shadows in the cold desert night

EL NORTE

Dust swirling around six headlights
Bright, glaring, blinding
White SUVs
A surrounding darkness
Lights from vehicle spotlights also
Red/blue lights flashing in the desert
Shadowy glimpses of organ pipe cacti and sage brush
Casting weird shadows
BORDER PATROL in white lettering within green bands

Green uniformed men
Radios cracking voices
Indistinctive

Organ pipe cacti in the shadows
Beyond the bright lights
Enveloped in pitch darkness
Standing like sentries

Three men kneeling
Hands on heads
Illuminated fiercely
Pierced by the glare
Glowing in the dust
Under the glow of headlights and swirling dust
Two with baseball caps
Red and blue
Shadowed brown faces
Gloved hands cinching plastic ties

A loud engine
A helicopter overhead
Loud, whuffing
Another searching spotlight
A light moving indiscriminately
Illuminating organ pipe cacti and sage brush and sand

"Pinche cabron"
"Pinche migra"
"Maldita sea"
Three murmuring under breath
Indistinctive

Smell of sweat
Smell of sweaty socks in the van
Tennis shoes with laces gone
In the darkness three men
Hunched over drawn up dirty dusty blue-jeaned knees
Jostling from the dirt road in the desert
Heads bobbing side to side
Sweating

"ECO POR UN GRITO" MODERNO

A room lit by blazing glaring fluorescent lights
   Cold and nondescript
     A detention facility in El Norte
     The wee hours of a bleak morning

   "Mamaaaaaa!!"

The wailing voice of a small child

   "Mamaaaaaa!!!"

Only three or four
Wailing inconsolably
Her tiny fists pounding the small table

A uniformed woman murmuring
Indistinctive
Sliding over colouring books and a rainbow of crayons
To the little pounding hands
And the little hands shoving them away
Carelessly
Without care

   "Mamaaaaaa!!!"

On a shelf nearby
Children's books
Colourful books
Lettered child blocks
Wooden, bright letters

Some stuffed dolls
A Winnie the Pooh
A Mickey Mouse
A Donald Duck

"The Donald" Duck's eyes chewed out
Cartoon arched blue eyes
With irises gone
Face chewed up
With a perfect blue suit
And a perfect blue hat
Its yellow bill with white stuffing coming out

"Mamaaaaaa!!!"

A child's face in agony
Red from crying
Brown from the sun
Sweaty strands of black hair
Criss-crossing the small forehead

An "*Eco por un Grito*" moderno…
A child's face from David Alfaro Siqueiros
Crying and wailing
And inflating, larger and larger
A child's mouth
Becoming a great chasm of wailing

"Mamaaaaaa!!!"

Filling the room

In eternal absence

MEXICAH

There the white ghost of Hernán Cortés
His phantom pallid arm covering the naked body of
 La Malinche
Her brown skin, her dark nipples
Hand-in-hand, white on brown
Brown on white
Over the dead body of a Mexican
Visions of José Clemente Orozco
Personified

"Malinchista!"
Tongues wagged
Doña María
Virgin of Guadalupe
Visions of virgins
Visions of Quetzalcoatl

Smells of charred corn
Rounded tortillas baking on clay comales
Round as the moon

"Last night in your bed
Êramos tres
Tú, yo y la luna"
Thus spake Octavio Paz

Mestiza
Mestizos
Mexicans
Nueva España
Children of the moon
Mexica
Tenochtitlan
Mexitli
Let the great eagle eat the great snake

On cacti
On many cacti
Walls of cacti

"You are nothing to us"
They said
"You are invisible"
Invisible people
Non-people
Invisible

Moctezuma dead in feathered and golden refinery with jade in
    abundance
Stacking skulls into walls
Huitzilopochtli
Unbearable sun
Son of god
Bloody on the cross

Revenge for the Alamo
San Jacinto beginning of an end
By 1845 Texas ours
By 1848 California and Nevada ours
By 1848 Arizona and New Mexico ours
By 1848 Colorado and Utah ours
Polk's little war

Rufino Tamayo "dogs" barking
Approaching city of lights
In the ebony desert

The unforgiving desert
A Tamayo luna
In greyish haze
Sculpted black escarpments far away

On the outskirts of civilization
Dogs barking

MELILLA

We the "clandestines"
Planning in Gourougou Mountain
Drinking hot tea in the shade
Pouring into one glass then another
Then another
Until the hot liquid fully mixes

Joking
Murmuring
Laughing
Amidst blue shadows of the pines
 Pines bent from coastal winds and zephyrs
Amidst yellow fennel flowers with long green stems
 Tasting of licorice
Amidst the blue shadows of the cork oaks
 Twisting up and down the hilly mountain
Amidst the white rock outcrops
And varying escarpments
Amidst fig cacti, flat prickly oval-blades
 Splayed in green oblique angles
Coveted seasonal fruit

Plastic tents, light blue, yellow, and pink
Wooden frames
Housing spare belongings

Moroccan police burnt them
And we scattered, running
Acrid smells of burnt plastic

Some make it
Some don't
Some make it
Some don't

In Melilla fences are razor sharp
And many of them to cross
One after another

They glint silver along winding roads of Morocco
Surrounding this Spanish city
Like an Alcazar of Arabic lore
Like a Moorish fort of olde

Yet this an Alcazar of new barbed wire
Silvery and modern and obscene
A hundred cameras
Infrared detection
More barbed wire
More razor wire
Motion sensors
Watch towers
Endlessly patrolled
With SUVs
With helicopters
For the barbarians

A seeming imposing evil to this barrier
Glinting silver
Like a giant silver snake
Ugly and forbidding
All encompassing
Preventing

We the "clandestines"
From Senegal and Cameroon and Nigeria and Ghana and Sierra
 Leone
From Niger and Uganda and Somalia and Mauritania and Mali
We the "clandestines"

Many of them were bandaged from the last time
Many had cut their hands and feet and legs on the razor fences
The barbed and razor fences

The Moroccan military beat you with batons
Mostly on the legs and hands
So you cannot climb
Many have broken bones
One had concussion

He said he was fine
There was no medical care
There was no ambulance for us
They will not come to the mountain
He died
One of us...
He died

***

He was richly dark in blue shadows
A blue-black darkness and sable sheen to his skin
And he spoke like a preacher to the others
His ivory teeth gleaming

He spoke of courage
Of going over the fences
The razor fences
To Melilla

He was like a black prophet
He was like one of the "leopard men" of long ago
A leopard king maybe
His voice rising like a witch doctor
Almost to a shrill
There seemed to be some animus in him
He was a magus to these men
And he spoke as if reciting incantations
All the other black men listening spellbound

We cannot go back
I will not go back
Look where we came from
We have nothing
We cannot go back
I will not go back

***

They climbed the first barrier fence at night
Looking like a horde of spiders scurrying
Forward and forward
In the hundreds, they came
A swarm of insects
Over the fences and over the fences
Like cockroaches in multitudes, scurrying forward
Nonhumans to many

Helicopter overhead
Shining its spotlight on the black intruders
Guns fired
Moroccan police beating them back
Spanish Guardia Civil beating them back

And yet they come
They keep coming and coming and coming
In human waves
Fast, so fast
Over one fence, then the other, then the other
They keep coming

***

He felt claustrophobic
Crushed against his African brothers
In sweat
Clinging to a wooden sailboat without a sail
A poor man's fishing boat

They left at night
No more than a twenty-metre craft
About two hundred of them
Black bodies clinging impossibly to this boat without a sail

The outboard motor died
The Mediterranean Sea heavily choppy
Slapping against the wooden boat
A boat without a name
Painted in faded blue

A red stripe around the upper hull
The paint chipped everywhere
The sea heaved them up and down
People began moving nervously about the vessel
Trying to escape the claustrophobia
Too close to one another

Someone shouted frantically
"Don't move too close to the edge!"
"Stay to the centre brothers!"

They had no life vests
The black bodies clutched one another in the black night
The shores of Morocco, its lights illuminated the skyline to the
 West
A string of pearly lights behind them

And of a sudden the small craft tipped
And they all went sailing into the rough chop
The water was impossibly cold
So cold

The men yelled into the night
Like the many great Igbo off the Georgia coast
They went into the sea
More shocked than stalwart

Many paddling in the dark waters frantic
Yelling and screaming
Their voices echoing off the dark water

***

He paddled and struggled as best he could
Gulping the sea water in heaves
Panting and frantic

He yelled at the pearl of lights to the West
He prayed to Allah
He prayed for his wife and child
Looking across the dark water
Of the rough sea

He asked Allah a solitary question
"Why?"

HARAB

We are refugees...
I don't like the word said another
We are survivors said another

They had left Homs
They had left Aleppo
They had left Al-Raqqah
They had left so many other cities and villages
All over Syria

To many they had no country
Nothing to go back to
Many came with nothing
Leaving at a moment's notice
Packing barely anything
Not even enough to keep the baby warm

They came from

Ghost cities
Exploded concrete
Gutted
Hells on earth
Grey and white hollowed out squares of concrete dust
Heaps of grey and white brick

Cities like those found in present day bombed out Gaza
Cities like those found in the bombed out Lebanese past
And present cityscapes of many in Yemen

Like bombed out cityscapes from World War II
In Germany and Italy and England and Japan
And on and on

Civil war ghost cities
Forgotten urbanscapes
Of no human life
Of no existence

Of a nothingness
Human made
A human made nothingness
A human destruction

No life
Not even a dog barking
Bombed out
Hollowed out concrete slabs
Of squares and rectangles
Grey dusted heaps of nothingness
Heaps of ash
Ashen landscapes
With no life
War torn
Forgotten

We left
We survived

We remember the beautiful markets
With wonderful smells
Teaming with people
Selling vegetables and spices
People smoking in cafes
Drinking coffee and talking animatedly
The smell of fresh bread from bakeries
So many shops
People murmuring
Smoking cigarettes on corners
Halal butchers
The echoes of chopping meat
Picking up our children after school
The beautiful Old Quarters
Archways
The beautiful mosque with its dome
The Adhan calling out again and again from the muezzin
For prayer, for peace

Now all gone
Gone
No more
Now nothing
No more
Now all gone

***

We piled into the black rubber raft
With life vests—black, red, yellow, blue
Too many of us
Two thousand Euros to the smugglers for us
A thousand each for our children
The smuggler now paid
He jumps from the raft

And the Aegean was a cobalt blue
Choppy water
Slapping the boat
Cramped and cold
Claustrophobic
The motor stopped

My God, why?
Lesbos is so close

And a Greek fishermen throws us a rope
He tows us to shore

And we make it
On the rocky shore
Discarding all our life vests
Deflating the black raft
Lucky not to have drowned

We have to walk to the port
In the sun and heat
To take a ferry to Athens

To get on a bus
To make it to Macedonia
To get on a train
To make it to Serbia
To walk
To sleep in tents
To sleep rough
No food
No water
No blankets
No toilets
Among the trash
To be teargassed and pushed back in Hungary
To be abused by the police
To be herded like cattle

"We are human beings!"
   A woman cries
"We are human beings!"
   A woman cries

We need to go to Austria
We will walk if we have to
Hundreds of kilometres
To make it to Germany
   Freedom is there
     Freedom for all of us
     If only

ACROSS THE RIVER NAF

Smoke billowed upward into the tropical skyline
Mixing with bluish-orange clouds from a sultry sunset
Amidst swaying green palms

In a humid sweltering breeze
Smoke rose and rose
Red-orange flames rising in the green lush jungle
Across the River Naf

An unfolding multitude of tragedies
The untold miseries of so many
So many

Just an enormous haze of greyish smoke on the horizon
Seen from the western side of the Naf
From the banks facing East
Lines of swaying palms and smoke
The vista from eastern Bangladesh

Crying into the sky
An unforgiving sky
Echoing into the night
Horrid screams

And the Burmese military came swift and sure
Descended upon them
Like a horde of predators
Coordinated attacks from Burmese tigers
One after the other

Tearing out limbs
Cutting off heads
Rolling like brown coconuts
In the yellow mud

More like wolves than big cats
Purposeful terror
Unrelenting

They came by the hundreds bearing weapons
Armed
Sabre rattling
With dha swords
And with guns
With machine guns, Kalashnikovs
With knives and machetes and torches
And evil intent

They attacked the non-citizens
Who called themselves Rohingya
Who spoke Ruaingga
Who lived in the Rakhine state of Myanmar

We are Muslim
We worship Allah
We read the Koran and learn Arabic

And Aung San Suu Kyi was silent
Of necessity
The Burmese military far too strong
Far too dominant, domineering

Silent by force
Even she cannot speak
Even she

And the yellow clay seemed to melt in the pelting rains
Puddles of yellow clay

And women in saffron coloured robes running
Screaming in the night

They snatched my baby out of my arms
And killed it
Dashed it to the ground

Then four of them took me
They held my hands
They held my legs
And raped me again and again

They tried slitting my throat afterward
And she showed the deep brown scars criss-crossed
Along her throat and the nape of her neck

They burned my village to the ground
They burned women and children tied up in their huts
They took the men
My husband is gone
I barely escaped

They took men and boys and lined them up and shot them
And many they took away

The army piled up many bodies into military lorries and took them
away
Stacked them haphazardly
Their brown lifeless limbs akimbo everywhere

As if it were a crimeless crime
Denying genocide
Just taking the bodies away

They were all huddled together crying
Consoling themselves about their lost villages across the river

Some men wore beards without moustaches
Some men wore taqiyah skull caps
Brown arms wrapped around one another

Women squatting in the yellow mud
Weeping
Inconsolably
Brown hands over faces
Faces buried in arms
Wrapped around one another

We left our thanaka behind
The yellow paste to decorate our faces
Said the wailing women
We left our yellow thanaka behind

***

A Buddhist monk in garnet robes said he felt sorry for them
The Rohingya
He said he had love for them

His eyes were cross-eyed
Ogling eyes
He looked like a Burmese Sartre
His teeth were rotting
Black and white
Rotten
From chewing too much betel nut

Then he said the Rohingya are not Burmese
They are not citizens
They do not belong here
They are fake
They made up their identity
They don't follow our customs
They are Bengali
They are not Burmese

His breath was acrid and gross
And it wafted across the room like rotten meat
His eyes looked one way and then another
Like a chameleon
Behind spectacles
As if directionless
Aimless

***

Thousands of them
Now on the borderlands of Bangladesh

And the monsoon rains are coming
The great clouds will gather
Piling up in great black heaps
Piling upward
Thrown to the winds

Great harrowing winds

And the yellow clays will wash away
Into the River Naf

Where the multitudes wash clothes
Where the multitudes bathe
Where the multitudes drink

The same waterway where the tigers drink

 Where they all escaped somehow
  In crescent moon boats
   They came

 In great rafts of bamboo holding too many of them
   So many lost now

    Without villages
    Without homes
    In the crowded borderlands
    Without a state to call their own

     Crossing a border
     Without end

MANAUS

A rainy day on the *Dia dos Índios*
The sidewalk was crumbling and puddling
As people jumped pooling water in their bare feet and rubber
sandals
A kind of sidewalk nobody would ever repair

On that day, he painted his face and body with red-pasty *urucum*
And black geometric lines with *genipapo*
His headdress, *cocar*, was made of blue macaw feathers

And people stared at him as he waited for his wife and child in full
regalia
At the bus stop with the rain drizzling down
Even in this largest of Amazonian cities of over two million
In the Middle of the Brazilian Amazon
People still stared at Indians

Why should Amerindians still surprise these urbanites, themselves
mostly *caboclos*

But today he and his people would celebrate and dance the
Tocandeira dance
The dance with bullet ants in woven palm frond gloves and macaw
feathers
To initiate male *Sateré-Mawé* teenagers to become men—a rite of
passage
But their *Adventista* religion prevented them
—the boys, the young initiates—being stung
So, they would dance with empty gloves that day

And their brown painted bodies, painted in red and black geometric
designs
Would undulate in enraptured song
Under the light of a large blue moon
Sweating and singing in unison and stamping their feet
Even in this city
Even among the Whites, *os brancos*

Sometimes he wished he was back in the comfort of the jungle, *a floresta*,
Under the canopy of green everywhere, a virescent umbrella
Comforting and enclosing lush verdure

He remembered listening to the hooting and grunting
Of the reddish-brownish howler monkeys, *os macacos bugios*,
The males' large throat sacks distending and calling out
And the hyper chatter of Capuchin monkeys, *os macacos capuchinhos*,
Their whitish fur worn like a hood and cape on their black bodies
Or the shrill cries of the regal Harpy Eagle, *o gavião-real*

He remembered as a child staring toward the upper reaches of the green canopy
And watching how the light played with blue shadows like
An *onça pintada* playing in the blue shadows as the light filtered through,
the golden fur and black-rounded spots and soft white light
Illuminating the blue shadows of the forest floor

To him it was more beautiful than looking up at the central chandelier
And the blue-gold ornate ceiling of the *Teatro Amazonas*
That great pink and white monstrous neoclassical opera house
The colour of a river dolphin with its Brazilian-flag dome of green and gold

And his mind's eye wandered to the verdant forest
As raindrops rolled down the bus stop sign
And the rain cascaded downward
While condensing on a house window across the street
Where an orange house cat, *um gato*, languorously licked its white paw

And the blue light reminded him of the stained-glass windows he once saw
In the white colonial double-spired bell-towered church with orange trim
The delicate sapphire light filtering through

The Catholic Church, *Igreja Matriz de Nossa Senhora da Conceição*,
Where he once prayed with his mother

And he saw the faces of his wife and daughter in silhouette and cerulean twilight
And he wondered whether he should return with them to *a floresta*
And live in the azure shadows of the jaguar once more
And hear the howler monkeys and call of the harpy eagle
As the rain trickled down,

The water running over his bare chest making the *urucum* and *genipapo* smear a bit
As people stared at him, a *tuxaua*, the chief of his people,
While he stared at the house cat licking its paw
As cyanic light came through the house window

PART III

POLITIKOS

SECOND MILLENIA BALLOT

I placed my ballot in the box
Not really, in many ways placed for me
I placed my ballot in the box
Not really, I punched it, or so I thought

That is, those candidates with the arrows leading to the hole punches
Butterfly ballots
Republican candidates #3
Democrat candidates #5
Or was it #4 and #6?
I cannot tell if the holes match up with the arrows?
What about the chads?
Are they punched through? Are they dimpled? Are they hanging?
I cannot tell any more?

An election at the second millennia
Of the most powerful country on the planet
And unlike 1800 or 1824, it did not go to the US Congress
It went to the US Supreme Court
Just another decision? Another *Dred Scott* decision? Another
Homer Plessy decision?
Where was the *stare decisis*? 12th Amendment?

And there it was portending to darkness
Portending to the cumuli of great massive cloud formations
Portending to a storm of grand proportions
Imminent doom of Mediaeval soothsayers
The daemon possessed

Ominous and portending and growing
Numinous words gathered, gathering, reaping, reaped, sowed
Winnowed in the winds
Chaff long gone
Blowing in the dust
After the gloaming of the Republic

CHANGE

Brought here by force
  So many of them
And so many died along the way
Countless arduous voyages
  here
From West Africa, they came
  Captured shackled forced onto ships
Treated like cattle, nonhumans
  Their children taken from them, their wives taken from them
Working in the fields to death, death fields, picking cotton mostly
  Black raisins in the sun plucking white dust balls
A lottery of sweat and drudgery
  Toiling and toiling under a blazing glaring inferno
Mule whipped, beastly tortured, defiled raped brutalized, daily
  Captivity without end
Lamenting and wailing and singing songs of freedom
  400 years of bondage
Captivity and Jim Crow
  Another 100 until X and King
    Summing up the reckoning
      Another 44 to 44

And he stood there in the great forest of the nation
  Amidst tall pines like sentinels in blue shadows
The blue shadows shifting with his pacing
  As if forty-three others stood there with him
The light cascading downward in long shafts of glinting diamond
glass shards
  While these woods held their secrets
Deep in the blue shadows
  With light playing on the pine needle floor
  And its heaps of pine cones, carpeting the loamy ground of copse
covering
  Rusty pine needles illuminated every so often with piercing light
    Amidst blue shadows beneath the pines
      Their obtuse emerald needles reaching skyward
    Almost touching each other
    Almost

In stilted silence
Brown sentries in blue uniformed shadows
    He paced
These woods held their secrets—ominous and foreboding
    As if these woods knew
What had come before and what would come after
    From the azure sky beyond

A kind of presidency with Disneyland automatons
Each scripted emotion, each scripted and prescribed word
    Circumscribing reality
Mouthing words like a pop star
    To pre-recorded music
In "The Hall of Presidents"
    Like going through the clown's mouth of the funhouse

Yet echoing Fredrick Douglass all the same
    And in him declarations of Malcolm X
        In him orations of Dr. Martin Luther King, Jr.

To the masses
Change we could believe in
    Change what could have been
        Actualizing actual change?

And the flag unfurled
And the drum and fife played
    As if for the last time
    Limping forward
        While the ophidian hissed "Don't Tread on Me!"
    Hissing in coiled repulsion

An easy smile
    A calm
    A legal mind
Brilliant overconfident diffident
My brethren's plight cried Cornel
    Incarceration rates
    Poverty
        Nobel-izing peaceful passivity

Slain dragon architect of the Towers' infernal collapse
  Droning through Iraq and Afghanistan and Yemen
  Blasting Libyan desert dunes
  Collapsing within implosions of colourful geodic loads
Colourfully distracting
  Salvaging economic disaster
Repurposing recycling citizenry occupations
  Economic salvations without consequential repositories

And black swifts
  Swooping in and out of narrow passageways
Cobbled and old
  Buzzing cobalt obsidian flies, specks, raisins, spinning
Before impending tempest doom
  Blackened low-hanging
Cumulus encumbered
  With sharp aquiline words
Shrill cries of children in the wind
  Of former vassals
    Supplicant
    Encumbered
      And passing
      Between now and then
        Then and now
      A promise kept a promise wept
        A promise in the wind

FOREBODINGS

"And ye shall hear of wars and rumours of wars: see that ye be not troubled: for all these things must come to pass, but the end is not yet."—**Matthew 24: 6**

And so, it was in 2016 a divided nation
Divided by patriotic fervour for one or another
Democrat or Republican
Supposed Liberalism against Conservativism, and *vice versa*
And yet what?
An enormous silence, a deafening hushed public censorship
A bloated orange character—skin like orange peels—arriving on the scene
Rakishly strident, a devilish louche, cartoonish
Eyes raccoonishly whitish from sunglasses or sun-tan goggles
A sprayed-on tan and blonde wispy-comb-over hair in abundance
The overly long silk ties in business suits
Trading on his name like a P. T. Barnum
A name of all names for a megalomaniac
Adorning buildings in BIG BLOCK LETTERS
On golf courses and casinos and country clubs and apartment towers
It became after Barnum, "The Greatest Show on Earth!"
The reality show, and getting fired, and Hollywood name recognition
Or did Swift get it right? Were all the dunces in confederacy against him?
And rumours of collusion with Russia, and tampered elections
And rumours of affairs with porn stars and Playboy models
And payoffs and corruption
A disdain for the Deep State
A disdain for intellectualism
A disdain for the riffraff
And yet appealing to the common man
An unlikely billionaire hero to the many to the hordes to the multitudes
Yet proclamations of implicit racism
A melancholy about a lost White America
Making it great again, making it grand again
A reality show presidency beyond *Bedtime for Bonzo*

A hyper-misogyny hidden by hegemonic masculinity
A harkening back to White Anglo-Saxon Protestantism
Pedigreed 1% landed gentry and disdain for the lowly low-born
And yet a false embrace of the boorish and the uncouth, unlike
Andrew Jackson
As if his WASP insect class had not stung enough
Twittering away in his own tower of fetishized reason
Isolated
Tweeting about his detractors
A shrill falsetto voice broadcast everywhere daily
Reductio ad absurdum, ad nauseum
And so, the rumours of rumours about rumours about other rumours
Ad nauseum
Manufacturing consent of a national media narrative, government
think-speak
Narcissistic grandiosity and pomposity
Mendacity, mendacious, deceitful, disingenuousness, perfidious
Fallacious, duplicitous, false, Janus-faced, dishonest fabrications
Alternative realities on Orwellian scales
Our Huxleyan *Brave New World*
Final bombastic proclamations, premonitions
Vomiting on the Stars and Stripes
And blustering and blustering and bumbling along
Popular disunion with rumours of impending violent civil strife
Rumours of impeachment
Rumours of rumours about rumours
Ruminating on speculations about hearsay
And Revelations supposedly foretold of a hydra-like beast with
seven heads
While a gold-plated toilet flushed loudly roaring like a beast
washing away waste

PART IV

TERRERE

THE TOWERS

An impossibly blue day that September morning, cobalt skies, robins' eggs, sheltering
And the towers were like two giant and silver medallions, hanging there, gleaming
Of a sudden, a terrible boom, a lurching of the earth, a shaking of windows and window panes alike.

Passersby craned necks upward toward the noise
As if those pure blue robins' eggs exploded just then
Shattered shards of cerulean perfection falling downward upon unwary heads
A havoc wreaked upon the peace of the day.

As if a giant's hand had dipped fat fingers in black inky mud and ruined the silkiness of indigo silky sheets by deforming the sky in that way.

A smudging black, ebony stain, streaking heavenward
Hanging forever there.

And there, a gaping mouldering hole, festering from jet fuel, not from decaying rot but from molten steel, a fire's rot, yawning cascades of grey and black smoke.

And in continuous streams, smoke billowed forth from this gaping maw, smouldering in an upside-down waterfall of smoky bile, as if Vulcan himself had struck through this perfect medallion—shining, erect, linear—but no more—hanging onto sapphire sky—now wounded, now deformed.

The sky was ruined that day forever.

Its cerulean perfection smudged now with awful clouds of smoke—black and ugly, grey and crowding upward into sickening clouds.

What happened?
Nobody knew
Some said, "It was a propeller plane."— Really?

Nobody knew...

People stood below looking upward
Pointing upwards
Mouths agape
Hands over mouths.

And then it came, low, impossibly huge, threatening, a whooshing overhead roar like an enormous black condor monster with outstretched wings, menacing to vermin below.

It came without warning, swift blackness, so fast, and so purposeful, and yet so surprising.
   It came, all at once
And this time we all witnessed it.

I felt sick to my stomach watching the ball of fire, orange, and all engulfing, and huge, as if in some Hollywood blockbuster movie set on the other coast, timed just so.

 It tore off a piece of the other silver medallion and the lava orange exploding ball, flashed
I blinked in disbelief
It did not seem real
It could not be real
   But it was
      It was.

There seemed to be a collective sigh, just then, as if the whole world gasped, short of breath, witness to this, to this what?
   Our collective trauma as a nation
   It was impossible
      But it was
         It was.

There for all to see the two perfect silvery and shiny medallions, wounded
   There, wounded beyond reach
Impossibly so

Black and grey smoke, rose and rose, upward and upward, billowing in heaps, too fast for any sky making rain clouds.

The sky was ruined that day forever.

Not clouds of redemption but clouds of torment
These sooty clouds of foreboding
    Was the world ending now? IS THIS IT!?

Clouds now, of black and of grey, smouldering from heated steel, twisted gaping holes—and billowing smoke from an impossible inferno
As if two gateways to hell had opened up for all to see.

The two silvery and shining medallions, there in relief, as if the air was forced through a set of two churning bellows, flaming the fires, smoke in obsidian black and in pale-ish grey rising, rivers converging, constantly, constantly, upward and upward, pouring, converging, pouring.

Time stood still in those moments
    But to chaos on the ground
People calling loved ones on flip-cell phones and BlackBerries
Others scurrying in confusion like ants
    As if a great anthill had been squashed just then by some errant giant's foot

People running everywhere...
    Traffic in turmoil
To utter pandemonium
    Disbelief

Sounds of sirens
Wailing and wailing and wailing
Policemen coming
Firemen coming

Different sirens for the same destination
And these silver pillars, still burning, gaping for air from a ruined sky

Twinned furnaces

Thousands upon thousands of reams of paper fluttering in the air, falling, flapping, flickering, streaming, and quivering cascades, catching sunlight every so often against the coal-ish sky.

Who did this?
Who could have done this?
WHY? THE IMPOSSIBLE WHY???

***

He glanced backward reluctantly
  But there was no way back
  Not now
Everything was on fire
  People were calling out for help, somewhere, echoing everywhere
Screaming in Dante-esque torment
  The suffering and torture of the damned
  Those who should not be damned
  Condemned in their trapped innocence
Suffocating, not wanting to be burnt alive the heat from thousands of ovens, wafting, engulfing, everywhere
  This hell of the here and now
He would wait it out as long as he could
  It was an impossible distance downward
    But now he could wait no longer
  It was either into the sky or remain and become ash.

The sky was ruined that day forever.

***

As if Hades himself had reached forward and pulled the strings from a towering four-sided curtained stage
  A shiny silvery garment falling toward the ankles of the earth.
    It came down
      All at once
    And downward
      And downward it came.

So swiftly it imploded in stacks, one on top of the other, in stacks.
  A towering deck of cards
   As if its builder had removed a wayward card from the bottom of
the deck.

It collapsed, imploding in a heap, of giant, monstrous grey, dirty
black, ashy brown, whitish clouds exploding upward with such a
whoosh of tremendous force of blown up concrete and gypsum, and
blown up hydrated calcium sulfate, and blown up plaster, and blown
up asbestos, and blown up steel, and blown up paper, and blown up
glass, and blown up plastic and blown up Formica, and blown up
wood, and blown up marble.

And just everything, and everything, flying everywhere, flying
everywhere in great clouds of dust and debris, nothing like it since
the "great dustbowls" of the Depression.

This, the this, with its Satanic intent, an omega blow, a fission of
raw energy released everywhere into this blue sky, rendering it also
impossible.
  All charred organic and all charred inorganic—plunging, plunging,
plunging
   In free fall—plunging, plunging, plunging
    Successively as if in sequence
   DOWNWARD
    AND DOWNWARD
     AND DOWNWARD IT CAME.

And the sky would never be the same
The sky was ruined that day forever.

***

And then after a short time, the next one too.

As if Pluto had taken out its spinal column in one heaving jerk like
slipping out the central bone from a great silver fish, wrenching it
no longer useful, discarding it to the ground in one swift motion.

  It too came down of a sudden.

In a giant explosion upward, erupting upward and upward in volcanic ultimate force.

Billowing black clouds, grey clouds, brown clouds, a flush of thousands of white kites of paper floating and whirling in the clouds outward blackness into a nowhere with the cobalt now far beyond reach
  IT TOO CAME DOWN
   AND DOWN
    AND DOWN
     DOWNWARDS
      SINKING
       SINKING INTO A NOTHINGNESS
        SWALLOWED UP
         SWALLOWING EVERYTHING

In a freefall, as if in sequence, a domino tower, a giant's Jenga game, but evil in its implosion—from nothing childish, from nothing innocent.
  A piercing wound, jabbed twice, from some distant spear, into our martyrdom, not theirs.
Into an inferno of twisted steel and metal, of molten steel, of exploded concrete and gypsum, of exploded asbestos, of exploded marble, of exploded wood, of exploded plastic, of exploded paper.

  Those are our people in there
   They were there
    We know it.

Now, torn limbs, sheared off parts, bodily departed from once embodied owners, partibilities of wholes gone, taken apart, deconstructed, removed
Strewn everywhere and nowhere—and all of the pieces in a smouldering heap of toxic stench, smouldering.
  A scene beyond Dante Alighieri, beyond Hieronymus Bosch, beyond anything really
    But certainly, most certainly, beyond mere words
Heaping and wreaking its death.

  And the sky that day was ruined forever.

***

Down below at street level the world seemed at end
Armageddon, now, today, is it really possible?
And as the filthy dust and smoky bile had settled, as if from the
bottom of the earth, they came forward like a great zombie army.
They came forth covered in death ash
Covered in filth
Their bodies dipped in whiten ash—men's smart suits, silken ties,
Brooks Brothers' armour—covered in death ash
So too, women's business suits, sensible pants, dresses—dipped in
whiten death ash
They surged forward, lurching
Some moaning, some silent.

It was as if they had communed together for some Nilotic tribal
rite—holding hands, holding each other, carrying each other,
limping forward in dung ash
Ashen bodies, ashen zombies
Their eyes reddened
Their looks of fear
Their looks of bewilderment
They came forward now, as if Aghori Sadhus, after having eaten the
cremated ash, after having communed in some forbidden rite
together.

But these were no Sadhus—NO—for they came forward coughing
and vomiting the death ash
Spitting it up, sullen, wounded, and coughing
And they made their way slowly toward the Ghats of the Hudson
from those sacred charnel grounds.

***

But none of the death ash would be washed away that day.
It would remain.
And now I know why John Donne said it "tolls for thee".
It tolled for thee and thee and thee and on and on in that smoky
horizon on
And none of the death ash would wash away

It would stay, impossibly so.

And from below, as if from below the very earth itself, in the most cavernous depths, a chorus arose, higher and higher.
It rose to be discernible but cacophonous.
This chorus said, at once in unison but in cacophony, it called forth
We will find you, it said, we will hunt you down it said
We will find you, the you who did this, the you who did this to us
We will find you said the chorus.
May there be peace?
But the dead were silent.
And the polis was restless.

As the grey brown dust settled down on the empty skyline, shadowed, foreboding, floating in a sickly fog across the island
And the ashen death dust remained among us.
Red, blue, white flags unfurling in all places, bravely and mightily so, unstoppable.

And the sky would forever be ruined on that day
And "our" sky would forever be ruined on that day…

OS ÍNDIOS

We have seen this all before
Happening for more than 500 years

And they come and we run and they shoot us in the back
Then with arquebuses and crossbows
Now with pistols, shotguns, and rifles

We have seen this all before
They came like army ants running madly through our forests
Eating everything in sight
And nothing escaped...
Nothing...

They came in ships like mountains on the sea
And they rode horses with glinting armour and they had steel

And we ran away from them into our forests
Our mother, our protector, into the lush greenness

Far, far away
But they kept coming...

And the diseases came with them...
We saw our women and children and old people covered in boils
and pustules
Covered in red spots everywhere

We saw our warriors coughing up blood from unseen enemies
These enemies with powerful medicine
And our shamans could do nothing...

And we died, many of us...
Dead...

And now tractors have cleared our lands for soy and cattle and roads
and our trees hauled away
And our corbeau forests disappearing, burning in huge fires across
the long horizon

Red-orange flickering flames licking azure skies as a great anaconda
flicking its tongue at the blue
And our virid forests being flooded by great dams stopping our
flowing rivers
And some of us are angry but most of us are sad...

***

We hear jaguars grunting into the night
And shamans say all the stars will fall from the skies
Soon there will be nothing
No forests and no moon and no sun
As jaguar spots radiate and circle around and around spinning in
blue shadows into the night sky

There will be no us anymore
Forever and no more
Forever and no more...

PART V

NATURA

HURAKÁN

The clouds began piling up in great heaps in the distant horizon
As snow in massive drifts on an enormous mountain
   Piling upward and upward into the atmosphere
   As barometric pressure began dropping.

Animals great and small of the marshy wetlands sensed it too
Something ominous from the south was coming
Something ominous and terrible was coming.

A majestic great blue heron craned its long neck
   In the shallows of the marshlands,
   Ignoring the slight movements of some small silvery minnows
   As water bubbling in small bursting rounding ripples,

And cocked its head southward.
   And then, in one languorous motion,
   This great blue heron fluidly ruffled its grey-blue plumage,
   Spreading its grey-blue wings outward,
   Reflecting its span upon the silvery brown-black waters

And with a flash of its grey-yellow rapacious dagger-beak in a blur
of greyish-blue,
   The great blue heron wafted its wide span of wings outward and
upward
   And upward wafting into the increasing winds,
   Heading northward out of the southern bayous.

And the weather became more violent
   As waves began crashing along the marshy shores
   As lightening forked in flashes along the darkening horizon
   Along the darkening southern horizon of the Gulf
   A purple-bluish dark haze in the distance
   Flashing bursts of Thor's striking hammer
   Along the anvil of the darkening horizon.

From space, it looked like the vast gathering of white cotton candy
As if by some invisible purposeful massive hand spinning air in
gigantic swirls

In a giant swirling of white clouds around a moving concentric fulcrum
 A colossal spinning vortex as no other on earth
  Of great force and immensity spanning the entire Gulf.

***

Guabancex, creator, would not control you,
 To Taino, you, god of chaos, fury, owner of great winds.
  And on that day, we knew you by Katrina
   For Katryna, for "pure"
    Yet on this day and for those to come
     Pure invective and vitriol
     Pure cruelty and malice

As if the winds could speak as they howled across the Gulf
 As if the Hurakán god had a conscious mind
  Of pure energy and force
   Lifting the waters
    Surging the seas forward in immense locomotion
    Forward and forward

Under Poseidon's enormous whip
 White frothing equines
  Surging forward and forward
   In their hundreds
    And the winds howled and whinnied

Whistling and gutturally roaring
 As savage and giant lions echoing in the winds
  From the shores of West Africa and Saharan dusts
   As a giant jaguar god, night sun, Kinich Ahau, growling
   Restless, perturbed, and endlessly roaring.

And memories of Congo drums could be heard beating out their hypnotic rhythm
 More fiercely and faster and faster
  As if evoking the god Agaou
   As if awakening his anger
    As if evoking his powerful brother gods Bade and Sogbo

There once in Congo Square with the birth of our Jazz
  There in rhythmic Afro soulful hymnals
    Hopeful hymnals sung to the moon and son of god
      And to Moses to free his people
        Echoes of a long, long, time ago
        Echoing in the winds.

***

La Nouvelle-Orléans, Nawlins, the "Big Easy" to ferners, where
bars never close
  On that Saturday night too all of them open before the storm
    In this Crescent City partying into the night
      Swilling beers and hard liquor and cocktails
      In bacchanal revelry and in rhythmic debauchery

To the beat of Blues and Rock n' Roll music
  Many little caring about this city's historical significance
    Either to music or to the South or to the nation

That night not bothering to clear the city or the famous French
Quarter

Laissez les bons temps rouler

***

This same city
  Singing solemn dirges to the dead in processional to the grave
    And returning from the grave in raucous dancing celebration,
      A life celebration for the deceased, following Saints heavenward
        Striking up, "When the Saints Go Marching In"

Funerary jazz, a marvelous wonder only in Nawlins
  With its spontaneous musical eccentricity and oddity
    From bandleader in colourful sash shaking his flowery umbrella
      Blowing his whistle in bowler black hat
        With musicians dancing with gleaming brass instruments
        To second line dancing of gatherers and newcomers
        Tourists gawking at the colourful procession

This same city
Where hot-squared *beignets* are sugar powdered
And *café-au-lait* is served with chicory

This same city
Where you drink the storm, a "Hurricane", just to thumb your nose
at it
"Who dat?" "Who dat?" "Who dat?"
They call out to you

This same city
Of Jackson Square and Saint Louis Cathedral
Its triadic black-white spires rising with crosses
Its clock calling out time in a timeless place

From the Battle of New Orleans in 1814
Where Major General Jackson defeated the British
To its capture in 1862
Where the North took command during the Civil War
Against the Confederacy

This same city
At Carnival all week eating "King Cakes"—iced in purple, and
green, and gold
Denoting purple/justice, and green/faith, and gold/power
Where you hide a plastic baby inside the cinnamony-creamy folds
As a promise for the following year

This same city
During "Mardi Gras", metallic coloured beads are tossed from
parade floats
And from wrought iron elaborate balconies in the French Quarter
To a chorus of "show us your tits!!!"

Many revelers masked and many costumed
Some pretty and some ugly and most drunk
Metallic coloured beads wafting through the air
To be caught with a flash of breasts or some other lewd act

Gold, purple, green beads
 White beads, yellow beads, red beads, blue beads
  Metallic glinting and glimmering
   Some large plastic bobbles

Wearing metallic beads in strand stacks
 Like Karenni women of Myanmar
  A sign of beauty among Karenni indigenous
   But here a kind of lewd inebriated attractiveness
    A modern booty of drunken urban parasites and pirates
     Worth nothing but memories
      Or lack of memories

Many miniscule spheres discarded and left shattered on the ground,
      stringless
 The metallic coloured beads rolling everywhere willy-nilly
  Tiny spheroids of green and purple and gold and red and blue

Along with discarded beer cans and broken beer bottles
 Their amber shards everywhere on black asphalt
  Translucent green shards like exploded emeralds
   Scattered like flotsam on a polluted shore

And dingy sidewalks stained by spent food and drink and garbage
 Blotches of all sorts along with smudges of blackened chewing
      gum
  And florescent green plastic grenade drinks
   Swilled and sloppily dispensed
    Along with colourful plastic straws everywhere

This same city
 Where Black-Indians in multi-coloured feathers, magnificent and
      beautiful
  Display in Mardi Gras like single-coloured peacocks—dancing,
      dancing, dancing
   In tribute to Native Americans sheltering enslaved Africans as
      refugees

Africans who had escaped grotesque Southern plantations
  Away from labouring on indigo and corn and rice and sugarcane

Natives such as the Cherokee and Choctaw and Chickasaw and
      Creek
  Remembering their Native-Afro ancestors in song and dance and
      costume

Dancing to sounds of the brass band marching
  The brass glistening and swinging and moving with the march

Ornate costumes—red and orange and white and turquoise and
      green and purple
Featherwork so elaborate in simulacra to
Caribbean carnivals and the great Carnival of Rio de Janeiro
Bedecked with multitudes of costume jewels of rubies and emeralds
      and sapphires
Elaborate feathers fanning out in great feathered headdresses and
      plumed bodies
With Native black pigtails and Native scenes adorning the costumes

This same city
  With the Zulu parade on Fat Tuesday
  Of African-Americans, Creoles, dressed in wonderful feathers
    In white-black face with whistles—whistling to the tunes
      Of the accompanying brass band
        Dancing and dancing

And so many other parade clubs
  With their krewes and their floats and their processions
    Endymion, Bacchus, Orpheus, and Rex

This same city
  With parade floats both new and old
  Telling fanciful stories and fantasies
    Of golden Babylon
      Of giant green alligators
      Of Zulu kings
        Of fiery dragons

Knights wearing golden and white face shrouds in sequined
costumes...
   Arabic-like perhaps, honoured persons riding horses,
    The individual hidden to festivity
      Masked and gaudy costumes at play
        Playing with non-identity, shrouding in bacchanalia

Floats of gaudy kings and queens and harlequins
Women's bejeweled sumptuous dresses of reds and blues and
        purples of heavy felt
   Sequined and brocaded in gold and silver threads
      And masked and feathered and decorously festooned
        Tossing metallic coloured beads to onlookers
          To tourists and locals alike

The anonymity of masks disconcerting—a revelry eons old
   Of subversion and perversion
     Reversing the order of things
       Men as women and women as men
         Anthropomorphizing animals
           And cartoon characters

And shaking bodies lasciviously
   Imitating fornication everywhere
     In libidinous lecherous degeneration
       Twerking

And streets in the French Quarter smelling of stale beer and puke
   And in some places like old piss

The black asphalt of Bourbon Street filled with broken strings of
metallic beads
The swill of beer and cocktails and coloured plastic straws and
plastic bottles
From fluorescent Hurricane drinks and Hand-Grenade drinks and
plastic cups

Like some Jackson Pollock painting—splashed here and there with
plastic colour
   And shards of glass and swill and drink everywhere

This same city
  With some masks ornate with elongated noses at Mardi Gras
  Those you find in Venice of Olde and in the grand 18th century
      masked balls
    Some golden for the ladies and some black laced

And women wearing skimpy clothing
  And people stumbling around and slurring their words
    And dancing hypnotically in the bars to a roar of noise
      And cacophonous and deafening and obnoxious shouting
      All at once
And everyone having a good time

As if Bacchus himself appeared with nymphs and leopards and wine
      and song
As if they were all dancing around him wearing the vine and grapes
In worshipful reverie in dreamlike states and trances and stupefied
      hypnoses
  Drenched in purplish fermented juice

As if madly bathing in blood ecstatically
  The maenads tearing men from limb to limb
    In Dionysian drunken rites
      Laughing
      Repeated over and over again
Laissez les bons temps rouler

***

This same city
  Serving the best *gumbo*, the best *étouffée*, and the best *jambalaya*
Where the Mississippi ends and for many where life begins and has
      always been
Once a great amalgamation, European French and Spanish, African
      slave and free
  And Native American came to these crescent shores
    To make a living and interculturally share with one another
      Their blood and sweat and semen
      Creolizing and becoming one another
        Taking a little from each.

CAJUN COUNTRY

This place named after King Louis XIV
  This numinous place among the Creoles, the mulatto French-Afro
      horde
    And beyond in the hinterland, Acadians, Cajuns
      At once the finality of the Mississippian delta, its mouth
      And the wellspring of this world

A land of the alligator, *caimon*, black reptilian shadows among
      green algae patches
  In black-brownish waters of swamps and wetlands
    Beneath Spanish moss, dangling grey like elderly beards

From cypress trees with knotty brown knees, *boscoyos*, arching in
      shallows
  Where big-mouth bass gulp at metallic-turquoise blue dragonflies,
      zirondelle
    Where *wowaron* croak into the night under a low hanging whitish
      orb
      Bellowing in their slimy throngs to a dead illumed eye
      A glowing milk opal in coal-ish nebulosity

Where giant catfish emerge from mud sucking to gulp at swarms of
      mayflies
  In their hundreds flitting on black-brownish water
    Stirring up fish in their multitudes in rounding bursting ripples
      As sunning turtles plop off dead logs from some startling

And black moccasins wind their way over mucky-virescent algae in
      winding SSSS
  And white-tailed deer churn up muck and mud running scared
    Making sounds like sheep bleating

As wild boar rustle nearby, grunting and snorting behind a thicket
      patch of palmetto,
  Foraging for acorns in blue shadows in high ground under a copse
      of oak;
    The oak trees festooned with grey moss over the muddy gathering
    As a grey mocking bird calls out squawking at the racket below.

These same wetlands where Cajuns hunt alligator for their skins
These same wetlands where Cajuns once lived in stilted houses

Now with airboats, pickup trucks with monster tires, and satellite
    television.

Men's knotted rough hands gathering up crawfish pots
  The crawdads, mudbugs, brown-ochre, wet glistening in caged
      encumbrance
    Clinging and squirming with moving pincers in an undulating
        mass
      And replacing these oblong nets with rotted fish to gather more.

Where Cajun families gather and say grace in their Creole tongue

And kill hogs in a *boucherie* reaping for a vast neighbourly swamp
      gathering
  As blood drips from the hanging beasts gathered beneath in tin
      pots
    Glistening red and frothing in tiny oxygenated white bubbles

Where moonshine and beer run free and the Cajun fiddle and music
      pound out.
  And the *boudin* and spicy *tasso* and piquant *andouille* is served
      from yesteryear
    Along with *courtbouillon*, its soupy-stewy fishy goodness
      Along with smoky ham hocks
        And crispy greasy delicate *cracklins*
        Powdered with paprika and peppered in Cajun seasoning

And *l'écrevisse bouilli*, in heaps of steamy redness, golden corn
      cobbs, and pink *patate*
  And heaps of steaming white rice and red beans
    And slabs of yellowish cornbread,

As Cajuns swirl into one another, sweating and pounding on a
      wooden dance floor
  To fiddling and song, with the wailing of harmonica
    And melodious banjo in accompaniment
      Along with a strumming guitar and beating drums

And a red-faced man's sweaty tenor voice belting out Creole tunes
  As veins in his neck strain to the song

As see-sawing accordion organ-grinding out the rhythm
  Along with the metallic-scraping *frottoir*
    At this all night *fais-do-do*

French Creole song and *Zydeco* echoing over a darkened and humid
    swampland
  Into the wee morning hours
    Laissez les bons temps rouler...

KATRINA

This same city

By the early Monday morning hours winds howling like banshees
Possessed demonic forces roaring into the night
As roofs gave way to the power of winds and pelting rains
As windows blowing out
As transformer-drums blowing up in sparks and flames
The Gulf of Mexico surging northward in convulsions
Waters pushing through the great Mississippi
Waters pushing through Lake Pontchartrain
Squeezing and drowning between waters East and West

This same city

When the levees gave way
And they broke in many places all that morning
Brown water rushing through
Again, and again, in systematic failure
And the city began filling up like a bowl
A fetid bowl of muddy ugly oily soupy water
With fecal matter and pollution and stench
Where the Army Corps of Engineers had failed abysmally
As the storm raged water poured in
Brown water
And people were trapped in their attics
And their houses filled up with the brown stinking water
Water filled with sewage and oil and mud
And houses pulled apart like kindling
Some pulling up from their moorings altogether
And desperate loved ones holding on
But could not

Grabbing one another losing grips in rising water
Helplessly watching loved ones floating away
Pets being swept away
Desperately holding onto one another as the storm raged
On and on
In pelting rains and rising surging currents

"By 6-ish that morning the Superdome's roof began peeling off
Peeling off like white band-aids in giant strips
As if thundering freight trains ripped through the top
And it kept coming down on our heads"

"And the trains kept roaring overhead
Rumbling and rumbling forward and roaring over rooftops
And blasting out windows
And it kept coming and that wind was howling
And howling and howling
It would not stop"

"It was like the end of the world
And we all started praying"

"And the water started rising and rising and rising and rising
And you could hear the manhole covers pop as the sewage just
opened up"

"And the water was rising and rising and rising and rising
And we all started praying"

"Couldn' get nobody on the emergency line"

"I must've dialed 911 hundreds of times"

"That water was rising and it would not stop
It kept coming up and up and up
And we all moved into the attic"

***

"I remember being on top of the roof that day
It was a Tuesday
" We were wavin' anything we had.
Somehow I wrote 'HELP' on a white sheet
It wasn' very clear but I wrote it"

"And the heat, oh Lord the heat
It was suffocatin' that day so darn hot
We were on that roof for hours waitin'
We were all prayin'
So hot
Didn' think nobody would come."

"And we could see the helicopter comin' in da distance
Da red Coast Guard helicopter
Whop, whop, whop, whop
And dey lowered down da metal basket
An' I put my children in it first
At least they could save my babies."

"I looked out that day and it was all flooded
Everything flooded
Didn' recognize anything
The water came up to the roofs
A lot of the houses were underwater."

"It must have been ten, fifteen, twenty feet of water everywhere
to cover all those houses
It was unbelievable
Nothing was the same
The whole city was drowned
Never the same."

"It was all under water
All of it."

"Didn' recognize nothin'."

"It was like the world had ended
And we were all praying."

***

It was Wednesday that day.

"By then the toilets were overflowing

It smelled like shit everywhere
All of the toilets clogged
Piss and shit everywhere
All over the bathrooms
Everywhere."

"It wasn' human
We were like animals at the Superdome
They left us there like animals
There was no food
There was no water
And there was nowhere to go to the bathroom."

"So people just started going to the bathroom anywhere."
"And the heat was unbearable
Lord I ain't never goin'ta furgit that
Weren' no water weren' no food
We were jis leff
Dey jis leff us dere ta die."

"Ain't never goin'ta furgit that, naw Lord, ain't never goin'ta furgit
that
They just left us like animals
We were like cattle."

"The sun beat down on all the crowds around the dome that day
Thousands of them and thousands of them."

"Nobody could take the smell no longer."

"We yall had'ta git outta dare
Da smell was somethin' awful, oh Lord
Jis sometin' awful."

***

It was Thursday that day.

"I remember seeing all dem bodies floatin' aroun'."

"There was a black man faced down on top of a car in a white t-shirt
The brown water was up to the windows of the car
His legs were danglin' off dat car in dat brown water."

"People were floating all over the place."

"Der was womens and chilren
Just floatin' face down in dat ugly water."

"And da stench, aw Lord, da smell."

"You could see the outline of a woman in the tea-coloured water
Getting bloated just below the surface of that ugly water
Her white t-shirt ghost-like.
The slight outline of her face beneath the tea-coloured water
Another ghost."

***

That day was Friday.

"There were people covered in blankets just left
Just left off the Interstate, off I-10
Dead people covered in blankets just left in the middle of the street
There were dead people outside the Superdome
And there were dead people outside the Convention Center
Just left dere with some blanket on em'
Ain't no dignity in dat, no sir, ain't no dignity in dat."

"We were herded all up waiting for the buses in that damn heat
Lord it was sooo hot
Like cattle
Unbearably hot."

"People were faintin' everywhere
And people were dyin' too
Dere was no medicine and no help
No food, no water
Nothin'
Nothin'

Nothin'
Lord."

"People were dyin', literally dyin'!!!
And they was nobody doin' nothin' to help nobody."

"Thousands and thousands of peoples in dat Convention Center
  People dyin' and ain't nobody doin' nothin' for nobody
    Just people dyin' everywhere."

"Dere was no water no food nothin'
  Naw Lord ain't neva gonna forgit dat
    Naw Lord, naw sir, ain't neva gonna forgit."

***

This same city

"AFTER THREE WEEKS THREE DAMN WEEKS!
  It tookim' to dry up da city of Nawlins. THREE DAMN
    WEEKS!"

"An' I go back to my neighbourhood and I just cried and cried.
  It was all brown and grey and I didn' recognize nothin'.
    It was as if a bomb went off, a mega bomb;
      All the houses smashed up and kindlin'
        Wood was just piled up all along the streets."

"You neva seen nothin' like it."

"Neva in my life thought I'd live ta see dat."

"Couldn' recognize nothin'
  I just cried and cried and cried."

"Ain't never seen nothin' like that my entire life."

"There was no leaves on da trees nothin' green no birds nothin'
  Everything jis dead
    Just everythin' grey and brown."

"Then the firemen started going roun' the houses looking for
        bodies.
"Mostly dey spray-painted wit' neon orange sometimes white or
        some otha' cawlaw
  And marked a giant X outside da house.
    On da upper part dey put da date
      On da left quadrant dey put which crew inspected it
      On da right quadrant any issues wit' da house
        On da bottom of dat X was da death count."

"And so ya go down dese neighbourhoods with da houses leff
  And stare at dat bottom quadrant 1, 2, 3 or Ø"

"God almighty it was da enda da wurl'."

"And den it was da insurance companies
    Trying to get money out of dem
    Or dealing with FEMA."

"Ain't nobody coulda' believed it
  You put yo life savins' inta dat house and it gone
    Jis gone."

"Or you doan' git yur money back
  Jis like dat all gone."

"Not sure if they wanted any of us back neither."

"What's fa shore dey don' wannus here
  Das fa shore."

***

"And you don't think watching all those families dispersing
  All over the United States in the thousands
    And mostly Black families too
      You don't think that was similar to slavery?
        Separatin' families mamas and their babies
          And nohow to contact any of dem?
            C'mon man

"We're talkin' thousands of people all over dis country
And dey was Black folks."

"Now dey call us refugees
REFUGEES???
   Whas' dat
   All's I wanna' do is git back to Nawlins'."

"What kinda shit is dat? Refugees?!
What I loss my citizenship in da United States of America
Who you callin' refugees?!"

"Listen' I was bawn in Nawlins, an' I grew up in Nawlins'
An' I gonna die in Nawlins
   An' das it!"

"We ain't no refugees
REFUGEES???!!!
   You kiddin' me?!
   Ain't none of us no refugees!"

***

Rememba' Hurricane Betsy in '65?
   Naw
Rememba' da Great Flood of '27?
   Naw
Remember this!
HOW COULD THIS HAPPEN IN THE UNITED STATES OF
      AMERICA!?
This!
   How could this happen
Here
   In this country
      In the 21st century?

TRANBLEMAN TÈ

Ogoun angry that day
    The day the earth swallowed our land
Our people buried
Beneath powdered chalky concrete slabs of squares and rectangles
    toppled
Folding like cardboard boxes of concrete, twisting rebar
White-rubbled, moaning, groaning, helpless hordes
We prayed to Bondye
We lit candles and the winds blew them out
Where are the Loa now
We emerged from below the earth, having communed with Legba
    and Kalfu
Powdered in seeming dung ash
Like Dinka and Nuer brethren
Yet it was us who were herded
Prodded out from beneath powdered concrete
Broken and torn and buried, some of us undead
Prodded out with crowbars, sticks, earth movers, shovels, bloodied
    fingernails
Some of us can speak to the dead like the Bwiti of old
Some of us must dance with the dead like the Malagasy Imerina
Some of us managed to run out into the open
As ceilings fell upon us
As the great sky fell upon us

The earth would not be still that day in Port-au-Prince
It lurched like the sea, angrily, mercilessly

And everything collapsed
    My world collapsed...
        Our world collapsed

My world became black
    Crushing upon me, crushing me
As if Damballah himself had grabbed me and pulled me downward
    To speak with Baron Samedi

The world became a white fog of exploded concrete

Even the Houngans and Mambos were helpless and silent
Our true ancestors in Ghana, Benin, Togo, and Nigeria abandoned
us too

Who is responsible for this? The priests, the gods?
Who?

Was there no Asagwe dance? Was there no Avalou dance?
Fanmi mwen? Pitit mwen?
Madanm mwen? Manman m'?
Papa m'? Frè mwen? Sè mwen?

Where are they now?
Where have they gone?

Giant white powdered black arms reaching out of white rubbled
earth
Throngs and congregations reaching impossibly skyward into azure
nothingness
Our bloodied and splintered fingernails clawing and clawing,
grasping air
Buried for now screaming into unheard emptiness with eyes open

PART VI

BELLUM

BOTERO ON ABU GHRAIB

About his painted figures
  Always something grotesque and doll-like and blimpy,
    Balloonish limbs and puffed-up faces and rolling fat,
      Excessive corpulence like fleshy-whitish porcelain

His world of naked Colombian whores playing cards
  With men in suits
His world of Colombian paramilitary massacres killing fattened
    peasants
  Bloated figures, a morbidly obese Mona Lisa
  A morbidly obese Presidential family, a chubby and corpulent
    ballet dancer
A plump and blubbery Pablo Escobar dying on a tiled roof
Escobar's attempt at blocking bullets whizzing at him like black-
    silvery cobalt flies
  With fat sausage fingers

And years gone hence, forward on to the Iraq War
  A war begun with false pretenses and missing weapons of mass
destruction

Iraqis imprisoned at Abu Ghraib, a penal institution, a house of
    horrors
  Tortured Iraqi men, suspects of atrocities, suspect
    On the margins of civilization, out of mind, out of their minds

And Fernando Botero taking a *Guernica* stand

Iraqi prisoners violently deflowered of their manhood
  Made to dress up in women's lingerie, sodomized with batons
  Forced into compromising sexual positions, false fellatio and
    staged onanism

Botero's bulky and stout painted forms artistically capturing these
    captives
  Captives of mind and body
    Tied up in blindfolded piles, portly, fleshy, and overweight

And yet toned bodies of twisted torsos and trunks, bearded and
    moaning
  Naked and compromised and tortured

Piled like corpses and carcasses as so many Natives at Wounded
    Knee
  Stacked into ditches, discarded, disgusting black-and-white images
  Of a militarism out of control

Hanging by ropes with red-sack-covered faces, Christ-like in repose,
    grimacing, and stoic

Nude bodies splayed about the ground, twisted gigantic limbs
  Scarfed from sight, bloodied, tied up, throwing up

Behind the squared geometry of metallic bars
As rabid cartoonish attack dogs with glaring white teeth lash out at
    hapless prisoners

Forms beyond paint, mutilated objects of derision, of an eternal time
    and place
  As timeless as Hobbesian and Machiavellian humanity

Bloated, bulky, fleshy, heavy limbs with giant club-like diabetic
    feet, trudging forward
  Clubbed mannequins, bloodied, blinded, water-boarded, shuffling
  Walking out into the daylight
  Zombie-eyed

YEMEN

Black flies flitted on and off her brown body, off and on,
  And she did not bother to swish at them

Her eyes vacant and sunken deeply in their sockets
And her head seemed so much larger than the rest of her, lolling
    awkwardly on the stick neck

Her ribs seemed to be sculpted from clay
  As if a wire tool had carved them
    The skin translucent over the ridges as hide stretched for a
    drum
    Her rib cage distended grotesquely outward from her body

The ribs becoming her with her bloated belly rising ever so slightly
  Up and down with each struggling breath

Her black eyes were angelic with a far-off stare of innocence
  A waxen delicate face
    She was there and not there

Her brown-skin clung so tightly to her diminutive frame
  As if her skin were stretched over bone or over driftwood on an
    empty shore

Each bone visible
  Her bony knobbed-knees, her bony legs, her bony arms
    Bones with skin.

She was a living skeleton
  And she grasped at her taut brown skin
    As if clinging onto her tight skin she could cling onto her life

Her eyes were large, open-wide but ghostlike, the pupils dilated
  She was a cherubic skeleton
    Her hair so brittle as mere straw

There was nothing left of her

And the black flies flitted off and on her body
  Black dots whirring around her And whirring around her

Her helpless form just lay there staring into nowhere
  Into nothing
    Into a nothingness...

PART VII

FACTICIUS

PROFUGO

Where have we failed you?
Where have I failed you?

There I saw you in the doughnut shop, the mass chain, its typical
    pink-tinted façade
    Its typical cheap doughnuts
        Fried up doughy things and so much sugar

And there you were asking to use the bathroom

Just moments before, I watched you carefully place your belongings
    (all of them?)
    Outside on a child's pull-cart, mostly encased in black-plastic
    garbage bags

You appeared too young to be in your predicament
    You were bearded and one of your bags looked like an old
    computer bag

And I wondered how you got here?
    I wanted to ask you: why are you here? Why?
If only

Was it some drug, some opioid? Child abuse?
    I had no way of knowing , would never know

Your face then transformed into so many other faces I had seen
    Lonely faces and faces in pain. Gaunt and some toothless,
        Pained eyes. Days, months perhaps, without a shower.

I had seen you on median strips
    At traffic lights with cardboard signs and crudely written words
        "WILL WORK FOR FOOD".
There was certain defeat in all of your eyes

And of course, capitalism had not helped.

Why are you society's trash?
Where are we to carry you off to?

Had we somehow forgotten you from a recent war?
Had you not been treated properly for your mental impairment?

And we all just pass by and go along with our day
    And we all just pass by and go along with our day

PART VIII

MACTANS

TRAYVON

Sidewalk glistening glowing from bright crime scene lights
Scene illuminated from impossible darkness all around

Candies strewn haphazard along a wet path
Red candy wrapper on wet green grass
A child's lost crumpled crimson prize
Yellow, green, orange, red, brown tiny orbed pieces everywhere
    oozing candied colours from rain
Oozing haphazard running coloured patterns on wet pavement
Like a child's chalk scribbling on a forgotten sidewalk washed away
    by rain

Broken ice-tea bottle, glass shattered
Yellow numbered markers for bullet casings
His lifeless form, an outstretched arm, a grey hoodie face down

He could not smell the wet grass any longer
His senses had been taken from him
Red and blue lights swirling around darkened rectangular buildings
Illuminating building shadows in blinking red and blue
Serious men and women murmuring around the scene

And the President said he could have been my son
    He could have been mine as well Mr. President

They turned him over, his legs crossed, with a look of temporary
    resting
His arms outward and his hooded face star gazing

And only moments before screams into an ominous night
Empty, echoing screams again and again
Whipping echoes about the darkened buildings
Terror filled
Forbidding night
Mantled upon everyone
A cloaked struggle
A timeless struggle for the country

He deserved an Orphean serenade now
A wailing of Carlos Santana's guitar piercing the night
A B.B. King Blues song just for him
Not even the mocking bird sang to commemorate the moment

A faceless boy in a grey hood
A hood making him monstrous
A faceless monster

Everyone feared this hooded monster

And Billie Holiday sang, "Strange Fruit" to the wind
There was blood on the cross and blood on the leaves
There was a cross burning to illuminate this banal scene

A vigilante assumed he was guilty
Just as those many White men arrested those faceless Black many
Accused of non-crimes
Put in chain gangs
And the faceless many sang "Lightening Long John" into the ebony
     night
Sounds of clanking chains in unison

It was no "Dry September" but it could have been
Rather a wet February night
A balmy humid Florida night, a Southern night
And if he could speak
He would have said, "I ain't done nothin' wrong"
Like so many faceless many black shadowed faces before him

Who will give our "Amazing Grace" now?
And I heard sister Maya Angelou say, "I know why the caged bird
     sings"
And I heard brother Cornel West cry to the masses, "how does race
     matter?"

I could hear the many sing in chorus picking the white clumpy balls
     of cotton
Tired limbs, dragging heavy burlap sacks
"We are climbing, climbing Jacob's ladder, climbing

Jacob's ladder, soldiers of the cross"
The faceless black faces mournfully sang

And all we could do was to look heavenward
Where those clumps of cotton balls seemed to float outward into the
darkness now
Like white embers flinging outward from this great bonfire
Comets flung across a night sky

Into the night they went
      Into the night they sang

As the faceless millions of stars illuminating that great dark dome

      Into the night, into the darkness, they sang

Faceless and black
      Faceless and black...

MR BROWN

All those brown bodies
All those brown bodies sweating in the sun
And Marvin Gaye cried out, "What's going on?"
We ain't got no pain Lord
Demons, brutes, animals
Keep working Lord
All these brown bodies
Lying all about
All these brown bodies sweating in the sun Lord
Whip your words Lord
Whip them good Lord
All these brown bodies in pain
And brother Frederick cried out, "If there is no struggle, there is no progress"
All these brown bodies crying out in the sun
The overbearing sun

***

Oh brother Malcolm, "I am for truth"
All these brown bodies
"I am for justice"
All these brown bodies
"No matter who it is for"
All of our brown bodies
"No matter who tells it"
Our brown bodies Lord

***

He was an unarmed teen Lord
Another brown body Lord
He bled out on the asphalt for hours Lord
The hot black asphalt
And Muddy Waters sang he was a "Mannish Boy"
The policeman's shadow dark and foreboding, longish, and black stood over the boy
It stretched out over the brown boy, Mr. Brown

The long black shadow over the boy's body
In the black shadow you could see the holstered gun
In the black shadow you could see the flat cap hat
In the black shadow you could see the hands on the hips
It was thinnish and long and black, shadowed over Mr. Brown
It distorted Mr. Brown
It distorted the policeman too
Law and order Lord
Chaos Lord
And Blind Willie Johnson cried out, "Jesus make up my dyin' bed"
And brother Martin said, "Darkness cannot drive out darkness"

***

Sometimes the men in blue are good men
But the Man ain't never good Lord
All those blue men in blue uniforms
All those Blues men
All those brown bodies Lord
"The sky is crying" sang out B. B. Coleman
And brother Martin said, "The time is always ripe to do right"

***

"He was a bad guy," said the man in blue
Said the Man
Another brown body Lord
Not every shooting is race
Black on White
White on Black
Men in blue
Blue on brown
Brown on blue
All our brown bodies Lord

***

In Ferguson they say
Dred Scott they said
Some Compromise in 1820 they said

All those brown bodies they saw
All those brown bodies they see

***

Dispatch crackled
Murmuring voices over radios
Sirens
He just lay there
Blue lights flashing
Red lights flashing
Dead on the asphalt
Lying there for hours and hours
Crowds gathered
Angry crowds
Shouting, burning
Shouting, burning
All those brown bodies Lord
All our brown bodies Lord
All those blue bodies
All those Blues men oh Lord

***

They called us N
He called me N
Damn the N
Those damn N
You damn N
We the damned N

***

And Howlin' Wolf sang out, "Poor boy"
Just another brown body
Blues bodies
Police bodies
Mr. Brown there in Ferguson
All those brown bodies
All our brown bodies

***

"Boom Boom" sang Johnny Lee Hooker
And they shot him down.
My brown body Lord
Oh, my brown body Lord
Ahhh Lord my body
Whip the words Lord
Whip em good Lord
My brown body
Lord

PARKLAND

Ashes! Ashes! We all fall down
  The green lawns perfectly manicured that day
    As they were most days
      Houses in perfect rows
A day just as any other, azure and cerulean skies
    Palm trees swaying in a light breeze
For this is a land of a river of grass, Pah-ha-yo-kee
  Where black alligators cruise black waterways
    Al-la-pat-tah and wee-lus-tee
A day for young love, heart cards given out, red decorations
  Some plans for romantic rendezvous
On that day some unseen arm was cranking a Jack-in-the-Box
  He cranked and cranked
    And tinny sounds of "pop goes the weasel" played out
      Everywhere

Ruinous sounds,
  Everywhere
    As a great metal claw across a black, black, blackboard
      Scraping painfully
        Again and again
          On the blackness
Ring around the rosie, pocket full of posies

                              ***

We were just sitting in class
  I was working on a project
And then it began
POP! POP! POP! POP! POP! POP! POP! POP! POP! POP! POP!
Then my friend just shoved me
  Out of the way
We all started screaming
  We ran for cover
    Panicked swearing
My friend said use books to cover your face
  To stop the bullets
Aphrodite was shot that day

Many times
Eros was shot that day
Many times
An innocence gone
And taken away
Forever

Forcefully so
Mechanically, ignorantly
Thoughtless

Seventeen in all
Girls, boys, women, men
Each deserving
Their own white crosses
Their own white stars of David
Their own white mala beads
Their own white crescent moons
Their own lives

As blood pooled on white faux-marble vinyl flooring
Huddling and screaming
Texting in closets
Texting to parents
Texting to siblings
Texting to friends

As the AR-15 fired without end
The muzzle blowing out the window slots of different doorways
Aiming at us
All of us

As the mad boy would not stop
Cranking the crank, cranking the crank
As pop goes the weasel
Vermin boy
Devil
Shunned
Psychotic
When will this end? When will this end? When will this end?

PART IX

OMEGA

OMEGA

And clouds slowly formed on the far horizon
    Heaping one on top of the other
    Like snow drifts on a mountainside
The azure and cerulean skies clouding over the great expanse of
water
    At times aqua at times cobalt at times black

On that day the waters were still and glassy
    As gigantic clouds became grayish then black
        Obsidian, smoky, low-hanging
Pregnant with forebodings

In the far distance in a purplish-haze the rains came down
    From the distance looking like watchet slate and slate gray
    Streaming downward in a limited rectangular sheet northward

Seas pavonated until the sun submerged in cotton shadows

And the cumulus rose crescendoing on the horizon
    Great atrous clouds expanding expanding expanding
        Intensity in motion

NOTES ON THE POEMS

FINES
The poems in this section were originally conceived as one epic poem about the "Great Migration Crisis". However, I was encouraged to break the one long poem into several. Hence, there is now a series of four poems about the US/Mexico Border: "The Crossing", "El Norte", "Eco por un Grito Moderno", and "Mexicah", followed by poems about refugee situations around the world: "Melilla" (the Spanish-autonomous city in North Africa surrounded by Morocco and a focus for African illegal-migration), "Harab" (Escape or Flight from the Civil War in Syria to Europe), and "Across the River Naf" (about the Rohingya genocide in Myanmar and their forced migration to Bangladesh).

The Crossing
The Sonora: The Sonoran Desert (in Spanish, *El Desierto de Sonora*) is an area of approximately 260,000 square kilometres, part of the Southwestern United States in Arizona, California, and Northwestern Mexico of Baja California and Baja California Sur.

El Norte
El Norte (Spanish for "The North"): often signifies the United States, the destination for illegal immigrants coming from Mexico and Central America.

Mexicah
In the Nahuatl indigenous language, "Mexicah" also refers to the "Mexicas" or the Aztecs, the rulers of Central Mexico prior to the arrival of the Spanish conquistadors. It is where the name, "Mexico", comes from.

Hernán Cortés (1485-1547): the Spanish conquistador, who led Spaniards in the conquest of the Aztecs (1519-1521).

La Malinche (1496-1529): Cortés' personal interpreter and also his lover.

José Clemente Orozco (1883-1949): Mexican artist and muralist. One of his most famous paintings is "Cortés and La Malinche" (1926), depicting the conquistador and his translator/lover naked, sitting over the body of a "mestizo" (see note below).

"Malinchista" (Spanish): refers to someone who is disloyal, a "disloyal compatriot", especially in Mexico. The following few lines contain a play on names, referring both to Doña Maria, or La Malinche, and then to the Virgin Mary.

The Virgin of Guadalupe: the Virgin Mary supposedly appeared to a Mexican peasant, Juan Diego, in 1531, in Guadalupe, a suburb of present-day Mexico City.

Quetzalcoatl: Nahuatl name for the Aztec god, or the "feathered serpent god", and a common deity throughout ancient Mesoamerica among many different Pre-Columbian peoples.

A *comal* (from Nahuatl *comali*) is a flat, smooth, griddle, originally made of clay (later, cookware using cast-iron), used to toast tortillas.

Octavio Paz (1914-1998): Mexican poet, awarded the Nobel Prize for Literature in 1990. I partly translate, partly quote the following lines from his poem, "Maithuna" (1964): "*Anoche en tu cama, éramos tres: tu yo la luna...*" A full translation of these lines from Spanish would read, "Last night in your bed, we were three: you, me and the moon..."

Mestizos are the ethnic mixtures of Spanish Europeans with Native indigenous peoples.

Nueva España (or "New Spain") (1521-1821), or the Viceroyalty of New Spain: included all of Mexico, all of Central America, and most of the present-day United States west of the Mississippi River, as well as present-day Florida, Cuba, and the Dominican Republic and Haiti, and other Caribbean islands, northern portions of South America, and the Philippines.

Tenochtitlan: the island capital of the Aztecs built on Lake Texcoco in central Mexico, the present-day, Mexico City.

Mexitli: a founder deity, and warrior leader. It is claimed that when the Aztecs changed their name, their choice was the Mexica or Mexicah in honour of him.

The eagle eating a snake on top of a cactus: this became the symbol of Mexico and refers to the Aztec foundation myth, a good omen, which the Aztecs took to indicate where they were to found their city, Tenochtitlan. This symbol is depicted on the contemporary Mexican national flag.

Moctezuma II (1466-1520): ruler of the Aztecs, prior to his murder and the conquest of his people by the Spanish conquistador, Hernán Cortés, and his Spanish cohort, along with indigenous enemies of the Aztecs.

Huitzilopochtli: Nahuatl name for the Aztec sun and war god.

The Battle of the Alamo (1836): fought between Texas settlers and the Mexican military at a Spanish mission site in present day San Antonio, Texas.

"Polk's Little War": nickname for the Mexican-American War (1846-1848). Also refers to the 11th US President James K. Polk (1795-1849). It was during this war that much of the western United States was acquired, as referred to in the poem, fulfilling the "Manifest Destiny" ambitions of Polk for US control of the territories west of the Mississippi River. The notion of "Manifest Destiny", a phrase coined by US journalist John O'Sullivan (1814-1895), was that the United States had the God-given right to conquer the lands west of the Mississippi River, and that "Providence" was on the side of US-white settlers of European descent in doing so.

Rufino Tamayo (1899-1991): Mexican artist, known for his surrealist style. The poem refers to his well-known series of paintings of dogs barking at the moon.

Melilla
Melilla is a Spanish-autonomous city, located on the Mediterranean in northern Africa, surrounded by present-day Morocco. Along with the city-state of Ceuta also in North Africa, and also surrounded by Morocco, Melilla has become a focus of African migration. This European city-zone is a favourite destination for African asylum seekers, attracting Africans from all across the African continent.

Clandestines: the name many African refugees use to refer to themselves, especially those hoping to cross into Melilla for asylum and to be admitted into the European Union through this Spanish-autonomous city.

Gourougou Mountain: mountain above the north-African and Spanish-autonomous city of Melilla.

Alcazar: a Spanish palace or fortress of Moorish origin.

Leopard men: The leopard, like the lion, was a symbol of power and kingship among such African Kingdoms as Benin, Dahomey, and Yoruba-land in West Africa, as well as elsewhere in sub-Saharan Africa.

Witch doctor: diviner and healer, known among many sub-Saharan African cultures and peoples; equivalent to a shaman in the Americas.

"Like the many great Igbo off the Georgia coast": there is historical evidence for the mass suicide of West African Igbo captives on the Georgian coast of the United States in 1803. Instead of succumbing to slavery, about a dozen Igbo captives walked into a coastal swamp and drowned themselves. (See: https://en.wikipedia.org/wiki/Igbo_Landing.)

Allah: the name for God among the Muslim faithful.

Harab
Harab (Arabic): escape, flight.

Homs, Aleppo, Al-Raqqah: cities in Syria.

Syria: The Syrian Civil War began in 2011 and is ongoing at the time of writing. To date, almost four million persons have fled the conflict.

Halal (Arabic for, "permissible"): used to denote food prepared according to Muslim religious law.

Adhan: the Muslim call to ritual prayer.

Muezzin: is the man who calls Muslims to prayer.

Aegean Sea: part of the Mediterranean Sea between present-day Greece and Turkey and bounded by the islands of Crete and Rhodes to the South, and to the North, is linked to Black Sea through the Bosphorus Strait.

Across the River Naf
This poem describes what has been claimed as the genocide of the Rohingya which began in 2016 and is ongoing at the time of writing. The Rohingya—a Muslim minority population living in Myanmar (formerly Burma)—are widely reported to have been persecuted by the Myanmar government and military. As many as 700,000 Rohingya have fled from Myanmar.

The River Naf: defines the southern national borders between Bangladesh and Myanmar.

The "dha" sword: common in Burma (Myanmar) and throughout Southeast Asia.

Aung San Suu Kyi: Burmese political activist and politician, awarded the Nobel Peace Prize in 1991. She has been accused of inaction and silence in face of the Rohingya crisis and genocide in Myanmar.

"taqiyah" cap: rounded skull cap worn by Muslim men throughout South Asia.

"Thanaka": yellowish-paste derived from the tree *Hesperethusa crenulata*. Used to protect the skin and as make-up in Myanmar.

"A Buddhist monk": It is thought that Burmese Buddhist extremists began the genocide of the Rohingya people in 2016 and that they have continued to persecute the Rohingya up to the present.

Manaus

The poem, 'Manaus', is meant to underline the issue of "internal migration" of populations in our world in contrast to the other types of migrations portrayed in Part II: FINES (Borders, Borderlands). In our world today, many people are forced to migrate internally within their own countries. Often these so-called "forced migrations" are due to conflict, such as civil war, or man-made famine e.g. Sudan, Syria, etc. In other cases, people migrate for economic, educational, and health reasons as many Amerindian peoples do in Brazil. The Amerindian peoples I studied in Brazil with a Fulbright Grant are considered to be urban Amerindians, for example, those living in the city of Manaus of the Amazonas State. The indigenous-ethnic groups I spoke to and worked with in Brazil were from eight different peoples: Apurinã, Kambeba, Kokama, Munduruku, Mura, Sateré-Mawé, Tikuna, and Tukano. Urbanized Indians are not recognized by the state because they are considered to be "civilized" (*civilizados*) and thereby because of their internal migration to cities lose their indigenous status. This is pejorative however. And yet, it means they may not receive benefits from the state if they leave the interior of the country. So, many indigenous peoples migrate internally today to cities for jobs, for education, for health reasons, and as a consequence in most cases live in dire poverty and on the margins within cities. One might think moving to cities has its benefits and to some degree this is true. Nevertheless, many indigenous peoples lose their language and sense of identity, unless like the urban Sateré-Mawé, they maintain their social rituals like the Tucandeira dance. I believe this poem, 'Manaus', exemplifies and symbolizes this type of internal migration. We may think of periods in history when such "internal migrations" are historically noted, such as the migration of the so-called "Okies" in the 1930s from the Midwest in the United States because of the "Great Dust Bowls" in states like Kansas, Nebraska, Oklahoma, and Texas, for example, during the "Great Depression" (mentioned in another Endnote here). Also, there was the "Great Northward Migration" (1916-1940) of African-Americans from the South to northern cities in the United States because of work opportunities in the North. Likewise internal migrations happened in

Europe after World War II. There are many other similar historical examples but too many to mention here.

Manaus: the largest city in the Brazilian Amazon with a population of over two million people.

Dia dos Índios ("Day of the Indians"): celebrated every year in Brazil on 19 April.

urucum and genipapo: the red paste of *urucum* (*Bixa orellana*) and the black paste from *genipapo* (*Genipa americana*) are commonly used among the Amerindian peoples of Amazonia for bodily decorations.

Caboclos: Brazilian persons of ethnically-mixed heritage from Amerindian-indigenous descent and Portuguese-European descent.

Tocandeira: ritual practiced among the Sateré-Mawé Amerindian people as a rite of passage for young men. Adolescent Sateré-Mawé males must dance for twenty or so minutes with palm-frond-woven gloves containing hundreds of bullet ants (*Paraponera clavata*) and must undergo this ritual ordeal at least twenty-times in their lives to attain manhood.

Adventista: practitioner of Seventh-Day Adventist Christianity.

os brancos (Portuguese): the whites.

a floresta (Portuguese): the forest.

os macacos bugios (Portuguese): the howler monkeys (*Alouatta belzebul*).

os macacos capuchinhos (Portuguese): the Capuchin monkeys (*Sapajus apella*).

o gavião-real (Portuguese): the harpy eagle (*Harpia harpyja*).

onça pintada (Portuguese): jaguar (*Pantera onca*).

Teatro Amazonas: opera house in the city centre of Manaus built by rubber-slavery money in the late-nineteenth century.

The Catholic church, *Igreja Matriz de Nossa Senhora da Conceições*, in the city centre of Manaus.

tuxaua (Tupi-Guarani): "chief" or "leader". Probably derived from the *lingua geral* (general language), *Nheengatú*.

Second Millenia Ballot
The poem is about the US Presidential election of 2000, when the US Supreme Court decided the US presidency in favour of George W. Bush (Republican) over Al Gore (Democrat).

"Butterfly Ballot": the name given to the election ballot of Palm Beach County, Florida, in the United States during the US Presidential Elections of 2000. Many voters in Palm Beach County were confused by the design of the voting ballot as to whom to vote for, especially elderly voters in the county. Moreover, because of poor ballot design, if the punch hole for the chosen candidate was not pressed all the way through, there were so-called hanging "chads" of paper and therefore incomplete votes. Eventually, the US Supreme Court intervened with an extremely controversial and landmark decision in *Bush v Gore*, on 12 December 2000, deciding to stop the voting recount in Florida and ruling that different voting standards in different Florida counties violated the Equal Protection Clause of the US Constitution. As a result, the previous certification of the election results by the Florida Secretary of State was upheld by the US Supreme Court ruling and the 25 electoral college votes of Florida were given to the presidential candidate, George W. Bush. Consequently, Bush became the 43rd President of the United States.
(See: https://www.supremecourt.gov/opinions/boundvolumes/531bv.pdf).

US Presidential election of 1800: this was between Thomas Jefferson (Democratic-Republican) and John Adams (Federalist), narrowly favouring Jefferson in victory, and decided in ballots by the US Congress;

US Presidential election of 1824: John Quincy Adams was elected president over Andrew Jackson by the US Congress. (Both candidates hailed from the same political party, Democrat-Republican.)

Dred Scott: US Supreme Court Case *Dred Scott v Sandford* of 1857 is considered by many judicial historians as the worst case in US Supreme Court history because it supported the view that African-Americans were not human beings but property and therefore could not sue in federal court. Another horrible US Supreme Court case, viewed as upholding racism, *Plessy v Ferguson* of 1896, supported the notion that as long as public accommodations for African-Americans and whites were equal they could be separated. Because of this, *Plessy*, supported "Jim Crow" racism and the racial inequalities throughout the Southern United States.

Stare decisis (Latin): "stand by what is decided", the legal principle wherein litigation may be decided upon precedent. The 12th Amendment to the Constitution of the United States was ratified in 1804 and decided the rules by which the US President and US Vice President would be elected. It was first implemented at the 1804 US presidential election.

Change
The poem's title is derived from US President Barak Obama's 2008 campaign slogan, "Change We Can Believe In".

"400 years of bondage": The 400 years of slavery in the US.

"Another 100 until...": From the end of the Civil War in 1865 to the time when Malcolm X and Dr Martin Luther King, Jr appeared as major leaders in the Civil Rights Movement in the United States, it was a 100 years.

"X and King": African-American Civil Rights activists, Malcolm X (1925-1965) and Dr. Martin Luther King, Jr (1929-1968).

"Another 44 to 44...": From the 1964 Civil Rights Act up to the election in 2008 of Barak Obama as the first African-American US President (the 44th), it was 44 years.

"The Hall of Presidents": Disney theme park show at Walt Disney World Resort parks.

Frederick Douglass (1818-1895): leading African-American abolitionist voice, writer, statesman, and former slave.

"Don't Tread on Me!": a flag used during the American Revolution (1775-1783).

Cornel: African-American scholar Cornel West (1953-present) an academic at Harvard University.

Forebodings
"a divided nation": a reference to the political circumstances and political atmosphere surrounding the US presidential election of 2016 between Donald J. Trump (Republican) and Hillary Clinton (Democrat), resulting in Trump becoming the 45th President of the United States.

The Greatest Show on Earth: promotional title first used by the "Barnum & Bailey Circus" and then by the merger of that circus and the "Ringling

Brothers Circus". The former began in 1871, the merger took place in 1919 and the circus closed in 2017.

"Were all the dunces in confederacy against him?": cf. Jonathan Swift (1667-1745), Anglo-Irish clergyman, satirist and writer, "...when a great genius appears in the world the dunces are all in confederacy against him." (*Essays on the Fates of Clergymen*, 1728.)

Bedtime for Bonzo: In his earlier career as a Hollywood actor, former US President Ronald Reagan starred in the film, *Bedtime for Bonzo* (1951), also starring a chimpanzee.

Tweeting: sending a message from the social media and networking platform "Twitter". This social networking communication-app (media application) had more than 321 million monthly active users as of 2018 (according to Wikipedia: https://en.wikipedia.org/wiki/Twitter).

reductio ad absurdum (Latin): reduction to absurdity.

ad nauseum (Latin): "to the point of nausea".

Brave New World (1931): science-fiction and dystopian novel by Aldous Huxley.

Revelations: The Book of Revelations is part of the Christian Bible.

The Towers
This poem is in honour of the victims of 9/11. The September 11, 2001 attacks on the United States by the terrorist organization Al-Qaeda caused 2,977 deaths and over 6,000 injured from a combination of events: the destruction of the twin towers of the World Trade Center in New York City, the attack on the Pentagon in Washington, D.C., and the attempted attack on Washington, D.C. from the hijacked United Airlines Flight #93. Approximately $10 billion in property damage was also brought about. In all, four airplanes were hijacked by Al-Qaeda terrorists, two of which flew into the World Trade Center, one into the Pentagon, and another crashed in fields near Shanksville, Pennsylvania.
(See Wikipedia: https://en.wikipedia.org/wiki/September_11_attacks.)
9/11 was the single worst terrorist attack on the United States and the worst terrorist attack in human history. Many historians and political observers consider 9/11 a "paradigm shift".

Vulcan: Roman god of fire and metallurgy.

BlackBerries: the most prevalent cell-phone devices used in the late 90s and early 2000s.

Dante: Dante Alighieri (1265-1321), medieval Italian-Florentine poet who wrote the classic epic poem, *The Divine Comedy* (*Divina Commedia*) (1308-1320). It is divided into three parts: *Inferno* (Hell), *Purgatorio* (Purgatory), and *Paradiso* (Heaven).

Hades: Greek god of the underworld.

Formica: hard plastic laminate used, e.g., for work-surfaces.

Great dustbowls: Farming areas in the states of Kansas, Oklahoma, and northern parts of Texas, USA, affected by severe soil erosion, which in turn caused the soil to lift away into huge dust storms (1930s, USA). Such man-made catastrophes caused many farmers from these areas to abandon their homesteads and move westward to California. This great migration was described in the novel, *The Grapes of Wrath* (1939) by John Steinbeck.

The Depression: The "Great Depression Era" in the United States was 1929-1941.

Pluto: Roman god of the underworld.

Jenga: a strategic game whereby players take turns removing wooden blocks one by one from a wooden tower. When the wooden tower falls the game is over.

Hieronymus Bosch (1450-1516): Dutch painter known for his detailed depictions of hell, his half-human, half-animal grotesque and demonic figures, and for depicting human folly and sin.

Armageddon: in the New Testament of the Christian Bible is where the last battle between good and evil will supposedly take place prior to the Last Judgement of Christ on Earth.

"Brooks Brothers' armour": suits of clothes. (Brooks Brothers is the trade name of an international tailoring chain.)

Nilotic: Nilotic tribes are African groups such as the Nuer people and the Dinka people, living near the River Nile in present-day Sudan and elsewhere in East Africa. Nilotic peoples were traditionally known to decorate their bodies in ash for aesthetic beauty.

Aghori Sadhus: Indian holy men who live as hermits near where bodies are cremated, or on charnel grounds, and cover their own bodies in cremation ash as part of their religious rites. They worship principally the Hindu goddess Shiva.

ghat: flight of steps leading down to a river in South Asia such as the famous ghats of Varanasi along the River Ganges in India.

Hudson: New York City is on the bank of the Hudson River.

John Donne (1572-1631): English poet and clergyman of the Church of England. The phrase, "for whom the bell tolls" occurs in his sermon, *Devotions Upon Emergent Occasions* XVII (1623).

Os Índios

Os Índios (Portuguese) "The Indians": Amerindians or the indigenous peoples of Brazil.

Five hundred years: Portuguese colonisation in Brazil dates from 1500. Genocide against Brazilian Amerindian peoples is still happening in Brazil today. Various cases of genocide against Brazil's indigenous population have been well documented.

Portuguese colonization in Brazil beginning in 1500.
https://www.brazil.org.za/portuguese-colonisation-of-brazil.html
https://en.wikipedia.org/wiki/History_of_Brazil

1960s-1970s genocide in Brazil: *Victims of the Miracle: Development and the Indians of Brazil* (1977) by Shelton Davis (genocide in Brazil during 1960s -1970s development policies under the Brazilian dictatorship)

Massacres against Yanomami Indians 1993:
https://www.survivalinternational.org/news/9455

Uncontacted Tribes (present day):
https://www.survivalinternational.org/news/12234
https://www.survivalinternational.org/news/12305
https://www.survivalinternational.org/news/11833

Munduruku (present day):
https://www.survivalinternational.org/news/12280

Killing of Guajajara Indians (2019):
https://www.survivalinternational.org/news/12268

https://www.theguardian.com/world/2019/dec/08/amazon-indigenous-leaders-killed-in-brazil-drive-by-shooting

https://www.counterpunch.org/2019/11/08/the-politics-of-denial-the-brazilian-president-and-the-fate-of-amazonia/

https://www.counterpunch.org/2019/01/07/preventing-brazilian-indigenous-genocide-and-protecting-the-amazon/

https://www.survivalinternational.org/tribes/brazilian

and the "Figueiredo Report":
https://en.wikipedia.org/wiki/Figueiredo_Report

https://www.theguardian.com/world/2013/may/29/brazil-figueiredo-genocide-report

(The **"Figueiredo Report"** was an investigative report published by Brazilian public prosecutor, Jader de Figueiredo Correia, in 1967. It documented and outlined the numerous crimes committed by the Indigenous Protection Service (SPI) against Brazilian Amerindians. This report also uncovered acts of abduction, chemical warfare, enslavement, land theft, torture, and sexual abuse—all amounting to "genocide"—and occurring in Brazil up until then. Notably, there were massacres of the Cinta Larga Amerindians and arsenic poisoning of the Tapuya Amerindians. The report was 7,000 pages long. It caused the replacement of the SPI with the National Indian Foundation (Fundação Nacional do Índio, FUNAI) in 1967.)

J. P. Linstroth 2015. 'Brazilian Nationalism and Urban Amerindians: Twenty-First-Century Dilemmas for Indigenous Peoples Living in the Urban Amazon and Beyond' in Michael Fonkem, ed., *Nationalism and Intra-State Conflicts in the Postcolonial World*. Lanham, MD: Lexington Books, pp. 405-451, for numerous present-day examples.

arquebus: early type of gun, which because of its weight was often supported on a tripod.

Flames: As of this writing in September 2019, much of the Brazilian Amazon is burning from massive fires most likely set by Brazilian farmers (*fazendeiros*) and Brazilian ranchers (*rancheiros*), where thousands of hectares have been destroyed this year alone. Moreover, there has been an 85% increase of these conflagrations from the previous year. Many environmental researchers blame the current Brazilian President Jair

Bolsonaro's development policies which aim to exploit the Brazilian Amazon and thereby have allowed for such massive clearing of rainforest to take place. What is more, Bolsonaro's policies have not only encouraged the ecocide of the Brazilian Amazon and mass destruction of its biodiversity but has likewise fostered the genocide of Brazil's indigenous populations. It seems Bolsonaro has no interest in protecting indigenous land reservations as evident by his administration's policies and his statements to the media. (See my recent opinion-editorial in *CounterPunch*, "Bolsonaro Fiddles While the Amazon Burns", August 28th, 2019: https://www.counterpunch.org/2019/08/28/bolsonaro-fiddles-while-the-amazon-burns/).

Hurakán

This poem was conceived as three continuous parts—'Hurakán', 'Cajun Country', and 'Katrina'—to form one epic poem about a devastating hurricane. It demonstrates, I believe, the complexities of a natural disaster in relation to a culturally multifaceted region of the world with many ethnic and social traditions, juxtaposing old and new, frivolity and tragedy, joy and suffering, and the human condition overall.

The title of the poem, 'Hurakán' (it could also be rendered as, 'Juracán'), is derived from the indigenous Taino word and name for "the god of the storm" or "the god of chaos", a male deity. We derive our word "hurricane" from this Taino word.

Thor: the Norse god of thunder.

Guabankex or Guabancex: supposedly the "supreme storm deity" and goddess of storms for the Taino people.

Katrina: Hurricane Katrina, a category 5 hurricane, which wreaked havoc on Louisiana in 2005.

Gulf: The Gulf of Mexico

Poseidon: Greek god of the seas, earthquakes and horses; brother of the principle deity, Zeus.

Kinich Ahau: the Mayan sun-god, who purportedly turned into a jaguar each night when he returned to the Mayan underworld, Xibalbá.

Agaou or Agau: a god of thunder, rain, lightening, winds, storms, and earthquakes in the Voodoo or Vodoun religion. As New Orleans has a history of West African influences, it is likewise associated with Voodoo.

Bade: Voodoo god or *loa* of the wind.

Sogbo or Soybo: Voodoo god (*loa*) of lightning, often depicted alongside Bade. Bade and Sogbo are associated with Agaou and share supernatural properties.

Congo Square: located in the Tremé Neighbourhood of New Orleans, north of the French Quarter. Allegedly, during the French colonial and Spanish colonial eras in the 18th century, African slaves were given Sundays off and allowed to congregate. This gave rise to African slaves playing music, dancing, and singing in these public venues, something suppressed elsewhere in the United States. Moreover, West African instruments were played and as a result of such musical congregations supposedly gave birth to the Blues and Jazz music traditions.

Moses: the Judeo-Christian hero who freed the Jews from enslavement in Egypt and who gave the Ten Commandments to the Jews from the word of God on Mount Sinai. Because Moses freed the Jews from bondage, he was also an important hero figure to African-American slaves.

Laissez les bons temps rouler... (French): "Let the good times roll..."; a popular saying in Louisiana among the French-Cajun population.

"When the Saints Go Marching In...": a "Black Spiritual" song of unknown origin. Most likely it originated as a Christian hymn but became famous as a popular song for jazz bands. It is often sung as a dirge at funerals in New Orleans. Its first lines are:
  Oh, when the saints go marching in
  Oh, when the saints go marching in
  Oh Lord I want to be in that number
  When the saints go marching in

beignet: French doughnut or pastry, a square of fried dough sprinkled with powdered sugar. The most famous place in New Orleans serving *beignets* and *café au lait* with chicory is *Café du Monde* in the French Market area, originally established in 1862.

café au lait: Coffee made with milk.

"drink the storm, a Hurricane": The "Hurricane" Cocktail became a popular and potent fruit-punch drink at the New Orleans Bar Pat O'Briens in the French Quarter.

"Who dat?": Cajun Creole slang for "Who's that?" This became a popular saying when the New Orleans Saints professional football team won the Superbowl for the first time in 2010.

Battle of New Orleans: In the American "War of 1812" against the British, Major General Andrew Jackson's victory in 1815 at the Battle of New Orleans made him a national hero. New Orleans was captured again by the Union Army during the American Civil War (1861-1865). As a city, New Orleans' strategic importance is its position at the mouth of the Mississippi River, and therefore control of New Orleans allows for control of the Mississippi River itself.

King Cakes: normally cinnamon cakes eaten during Mardi Gras, often decorated with Mardi Gras colours of purple, green, and yellow. In its folds are placed a plastic baby, originally representing baby Jesus. Anyone who finds the baby in their slice of cake is said to have good luck for the rest of the year.

Mardi Gras (French) "Fat Tuesday": name given to the Carnival celebrations in New Orleans; known simply as "Carnival" elsewhere in the world where it is commemorated. It is the tradition in Catholic Christian communities of eating to excess and indulging in gluttony prior to the fasting and penitential obligations of Lent. Carnival is likewise associated with libidinous behaviour and drunken revelry.

Karenni women of Myanmar: The Karenni-Padaung or Kayan people are an indigenous Southeast Asian people located within the Burmese and Thai borders. The Padaung women are famous for wearing metal neck rings which elongate their necks, in a way considered among them as aesthetically beautiful.

Black Indians: The "Black Indians" of the New Orleans Mardi Gras—also known as "The Mardi Gras Indians"—are organized into almost forty groupings of performing groups. They wear elaborate feathered costumes and renowned for their dancing. Their historical origins are associated with the admixture of escaped African slaves seeking refuge among Native American peoples in the region such as the Cherokee, Chickasaw, Choctaw, and Creek. Later, such freed African-Americans also served as so-called "Buffalo Soldiers".

  "Black Indians" and their respective "Krewes" (see below) may have their historical antecedence in rituals associated with "Moors and Christians", having to do with the Spanish conquest of the Iberian Peninsula in the Middle Ages over the Moors.

Krewes: a social organization that puts on a parade or ball for the Carnival season.

Endymion, Bacchus, Orpheus, and Rex: names of some of the more famous parades held during Mardi Gras in New Orleans.

Arabic-like perhaps, honoured persons riding horses:
In a recent article by Jeroen Dewulf (2015), 'From Moors to Indians: The Mardi Gras Indians and the Three Transformations of St. James' in *Louisiana History: The Journal of the Louisiana Historical Association* (Vol. 56, No. 1, pp. 5-41), he explains that influences on the Mardi Gras parades of New Orleans may date back to the Spanish conquest of the Moors in Spain during the Middle Ages. These influences are widespread throughout Latin America, and include celebrations known as "Moors and Christians" (in Spanish, *"Moros y Cristianos"*, or in Portuguese, *"Mouros e Cristãos"*). Various parades and "parade Krewes" in the New Orleans Mardi Gras may be traced to such Mediaeval revelry as well as the Christian veneration of St. James or the "Moor Slayer" (Mata Moros), but they also include some nineteenth century influences in the United States as the "Buffalo Bill Shows", e.g. the Mardi Gras Indians Krewe and Krewe of Rex. Such parade groups may additionally have some aesthetic ties to the Easter processionals in Andalusia, Spain (the hooded costumes are similar and there are Catholic influences on the parades and parade groups). (See Link:
https://www.jstor.org/stable/24396493?read-now=1&seq=1#metadata_info_tab_contents)

"Hand-Grenade drinks": a popular melon-flavoured cocktail served in gaudy containers shaped like a hand-grenade. These are sold in the French Quarter of New Orleans, allegedly by five approved establishments.

Jackson Pollock (1912-1956): American painter renowned for his abstract splashing paint compositions and a major figure in the abstract-expressionist artistic movement.

Masks: In the annual Carnival of Venice, Italy, elaborate and decorative masks are worn by revellers.

Bacchus: Roman god of wine, revelry, fertility, and ritual ecstasy. His Greek equivalent is Dionysius.

Gumbo, Étouffee, Jambalaya: famous Cajun and Creole dishes.

Gumbo: a hardy soupy-stew normally made with shellfish, andouille (a spicy pork sausage), and a mix of vegetables, such as okra, celery, bell peppers, onions, rice, and chicken stock.
Étouffee: a thickish sauce and spicy stew made of shellfish, normally ladled over rice.

Jambalaya: similar to Spanish paella, drier than gumbo, and served with rice.

Cajun Country
Cajun Country: area in the interior of Louisiana. The Cajuns, also known as Acadians or, "Les Acadiens" (French). During the so-called "Great Expulsion", following the Seven-Years' War (1756-1763) and part of the French and Indian War (1754-1758), French settlers living in Acadia (now New Brunswick, Nova Scotia, Prince Edward Island, parts of Quebec in Canada, and parts of Maine in the USA), were expelled by the British. They then settled in the northern areas of Louisiana whereas the southern portions had already been settled by French colonists much earlier. Part of my own family, my mother's French side, settled in Louisiana as well. (See: https://en.wikipedia.org/wiki/Cajuns).

King Louis XIV (1638-1715), also known as the "Sun King": King of France for seventy-two years, at the time of writing, the longest reigning European monarch of all time. During his reign, France was the leading European power.

Caiman (French Cajun): American alligator (*Alligator mississippiensis*).

wowaron (Cajun): American bullfrog (*Lithobates catesbeianus*).

Boucherie (French Creole): "butchery", referring to the tradition of butchering of hogs and the accompanying feast and festivities.

Boudin: boudin balls are often made with spicy pork sausage and rice and fried up in bite-size balls. At times, they are made with alligator or crawfish meat.

Tasso: spicy smoked ham-shoulder.

andouille: type of Cajun spicy sausage.

Courtbouillon: tomato-based fish and shellfish stew.

<u>Cracklins</u>: fried pork rind or fried pig skin.

<u>l'écrevisse bouilli</u>: "crayfish (or crawfish) boil". Crayfish are boiled along with corn and baby red potatoes or *patate* and normally seasoned with "all spice" or a Cajun spice-mix. The food is then served to numerous people, sitting communally at long tables. *L'écrevisse bouilli* is normally served on festive occasions.

<u>White rice and red beans and cornbread</u>: typical Cajun side dishes. (Cornbread is also ubiquitous throughout the Southern United States.)

Frottoir (often referred to as a "vest *frottoir*"): washboard instrument typically worn on the chest.

<u>*Fais-do-do*</u>: Cajun dance party.

<u>*Zydeco*</u>: Cajun music genre combining Blues and Cajun-music styles. It is dominated by musical instruments the accordion and the washboard.

Katrina
Hurricane Katrina in 2005 was a Category 5 hurricane, or the deadliest category with sustained winds of as much as 205 km/h in the city, making it one of the most powerful storms in recorded history. Its devastation of New Orleans was in many respects unprecedented. As a result of the storm, the levees surrounding the city of New Orleans were breached, which flooded 80% of the city for more than two weeks. Almost 1,500 people died as a result of the storm in New Orleans which also caused as much as $70 billion dollars in damage. While estimates suggest that 80 to 90 percent of the population evacuated the city because of the storm, many of the poorest residents remained, having little means to escape the impending hurricane. In the aftermath of Hurricane Katrina, the Bush Administration was heavily criticized for its inaction and ill-preparedness. This poem, 'Katrina', is dedicated to those who died because of Hurricane Katrina and those who suffered so much as a result of this natural disaster.

In writing this poem I tried to capture the local vernacular of New Orleans, especially that of the many African-American residents who remained trapped in the city or who suffered as a result of this devastating natural disaster. My capturing of the local vernacular and comments made by the people is based upon several documentaries about "Katrina" as well as several visits to New Orleans. In my view, the most powerful documentary about Hurricane Katrina and its unfortunate aftermath is, "*When the Levees Broke: A Requiem in Four Acts*", directed by filmmaker Spike Lee (2006).

(See, https://www.imdb.com/title/tt0783612/?ref_=fn_al_tt_1) It is a moving tribute to Katrina survivors and demonstrates, I believe, the racial disparities underlined by this natural disaster. (See also, Michael Eric Dyson 2005. *Come Hell or High Water: Hurricane Katrina and the Color of Disaster.* New York: Basic Civitas Books.)

FEMA (Federal Emergency Management Agency of the United States): It is under the auspices of the Department of Homeland Security (DHS) and is the agency responsible for responding to disasters in the United States. It provides aid in situations when local and state governments are inadequate to the given emergency (see: https://www.fema.gov).

Dispersing: As a result of Hurricane Katrina, over a million people were displaced from the Gulf Coast region. While many returned, at least 600,000 people remained displaced a month later from the aftermath of the storm. (These statistics are derived from: https://www.datacenterresearch.org/data-resources/katrina/facts-for-impact/).

However, 10 years after the storm (2015), the statistics paint a much starker picture of New Orleans resident displacement as a result of Katrina: https://www.citylab.com/equity/2015/08/10-years-later-theres-still-a-lot-we-dont-know-about-where-katrina-survivors-ended-up/401216/ . For it seems from demographic data gathered that only 53% of adult former residents returned to the city, while the majority of those displaced moved to northern Louisiana and Texas.

Hurricane Betsy of 1965: a Category 4 storm which had devastating consequences for the Gulf Coast and Louisiana. As in the case of Katrina, later, it also caused the breaching of the levees of New Orleans. Hurricane Betsy caused a total of 81 fatalities and almost $1.5 billion in damage. (See: https://en.wikipedia.org/wiki/Hurricane_Betsy)

Great Flood of [19]27: The Great Mississippi Flood of 1927 was the most destructive river flood to date in the history of the United States. In effect, 70,000 square kilometres and about 630,000 people living in the flooded areas of Arkansas, Mississippi, and Louisiana were affected. See https://en.wikipedia.org/wiki/Great_Mississippi_Flood_of_1927)

Tranbleman Tè
This poem is dedicated to the more than 250,000 Haitians and others who perished because of the earthquake in Haiti in 2010, as well as the estimated more than 300,000 people who were injured. The epicentre was approximately 25 kilometres west of the capital of Port-au-Prince and it had a magnitude of 7.0 M_w.
(See: https://en.wikipedia.org/wiki/2010_Haiti_earthquake)

Tranbleman Tè (Haitian Creole): "Earthquake"

Ogoun or Ogun is an orisha (god) and loa (spirit), a warrior deity who is ruler of politics, war, metallurgy, and hunting. He is worshipped, for example, in Haitian Voodoo, Afro-Brazilian *Candomblé*, Cuban *Santeria*, and among the Edo, Fon, and Yoruba peoples of West Africa. (See: https://en.wikipedia.org/wiki/Ogun See also, Jacob Olupona and Terry Rey, eds. 2008, *Orisa Devotion as World Religion: the Globalization of Yoruba Religious Culture*. Madison, WI: University of Wisconsin Press.)

Bondye (derivation from "Bon Dieu" (French) "Good God": a "supreme deity" in Haitian Voodoo. Apparently, he is a more distant god and does not interfere with human everyday life. Voodoo religious beliefs originated in West Africa among the Ewe, Fon, Kongo, and Yoruba, and have an admixture of Catholic Christianity.
(See for example: https://en.wikipedia.org/wiki/Haitian_Vodou
See also, Alfred Métraux, trans. Hugo Charteris 1972. *Voodoo in Haiti*. New York: Schocken Books.)

Loa are spirits in Voodoo which are called upon in order to intervene in human affairs.

Legba (often "Papa Legba"): Haitian spirit (*loa*) often acting as intermediary between humans and spirits. Said to speak all human languages and often associated with dogs.
(See: https://en.wikipedia.org/wiki/Papa_Legba)

Kalfu: spiritual aspect of Legba (q.v.). Commonly envisioned as a young red-coloured man or demon, usually syncretised with Satan; controller of cross-roads. (See: https://en.wikipedia.org/wiki/Kalfu)

The Dinka and the Nuer: Nilotic, cattle-herding peoples, who live in East Africa, specifically in the region of present day Sudan and are traditional enemies. They are well-known in the anthropology of Africa. (See: R. G. Lienhardt 1961. *Divinity and Experience: the Religion of the Dinka*. Oxford: Clarendon Press. and E. E. Evans-Pritchard 1940. *The Nuer: a Description of the Modes of Livelihood and Political Institutions of a Nilotic People*. Oxford: Clarendon Press.)

Bwiti: a spiritual religion among the Fang people of Cameroon and Gabon in West Africa. Bwiti, like Haitian Voodoo, is a synchretic religion which includes varying belief systems, including Christianity, African animism, and ancestor worship. One significant difference is that Bwiti practitioners among the Fang people of West Africa use the hallucinogen, "iboga", from the tree root, *Tabernanthe iboga*. (See: J. W. Fernandez 1982. *Bwiti: an Ethnography of the Religious Imagination in Africa*. Princeton: Princeton University Press.)

Malagasy Imerina (also "Merina"): a people from Madagascar. Their population today numbers some 5 million people. The sacred ritual among the Imerina of unearthing and reburying the dead is called *"famadihana"* or "the turning of the bones". In a cycle of every five to seven years, ancestors are removed from burial crypts. Their silk burial shrouds are removed and replaced with new ones. In the unburial ceremony, the Imerina dance with the corpses of their ancestors. The appropriate emotion is considered to be joy rather than sadness.
(See: https://www.cnn.com/2016/10/18/travel/madagascar-turning-bones/index.html
and see: Maurice Bloch 1971. *Placing the Dead: Tombs, Ancestral Villages, and Kinship Organization in Madagascar*. London: LSE Monographs Press.)

Damballah: the sky god in Haitian Voodoo. He is often depicted as a serpent spirit and considered the primordial creator of life on earth. (See previous works about Haitian Voodoo, referenced above.)

Baron Samedi (also "Baron Samdi") "Baron Saturday": a *loa* or spirit of the dead. He is often depicted wearing a top hat and tailcoat, smoking a cigar and wearing dark sunglasses with cotton nose plugs, just like a corpse. At times, he is seen as a Haitian man with a painted skull face, and at other times, he is seen as a skeleton.
(See: https://en.wikipedia.org/wiki/Baron_Samedi and previous references on Haitian Voodoo.)

houngan: a male priest in Haitian Voodoo. A female priestess is called a "mambo". (See previous references on Haitian Voodoo.)

Asagwe dance: a type of exuberant dancing in Voodoo rituals to honour the "spirits" or *loa*.
Avalou dance: prayer dancing in the form of begging and supplication.

Asagwe and Avalou dances are often done in conjunction with those who believe they are possessed by the *loa* or spirits of different Haitian gods and they are similar to "spirit possession rituals" in West Africa (see references above).

"Fanmi mwen? Pitit mwen? Madanm mwen? Manman m' ? Papa m'?" (Haitian Creole): "My family? My child? My wife? My mother? My dad?"

Frè mwen? Sè mwen? (Haitian Creole): "My brother? It's me?..."

PART VI BELLUM

Botero On Abu Ghraib

Fernando Botero (1932-): contemporary Colombian artist known for depicting people in a corpulent and oversized fashion. His style of art is known as "Boterismo" and may represent political criticism, humour, or satire. He is perhaps the most recognized Latin American artist of today. Abu Ghraib Prison in Iraq was in 2003 the centre of an Iraqi prisoner abuse scandal committed by US soldiers. Some of the alleged accusations were sexual abuse, rape, torture, sodomy, and murder. The public first became aware of the scandal with the release of photos to CBS News in 2004. (See: https://en.wikipedia.org/wiki/Abu_Ghraib_torture_and_prisoner_abuse). In response to the scandal, Botero created a series of drawings and paintings based on the alleged Iraqi prisoner abuse. Botero's Abu Ghraib Series is now housed at the Art Museum at UC Berkeley in California, USA. (See: https://www.nytimes.com/2007/08/30/arts/design/30arts-BOTEROGIVESA_BRF.html.)

My poem, 'Botero on Abu Ghraib' refers to some specific paintings in the Abu Ghraib Series. Botero, for example, re-painted the "Mona Lisa" in his own style. The famous "Mona Lisa" (circa? 1517) was originally painted by the Italian Renaissance artist, Leonardo da Vinci, and is now housed in the Louvre Museum of Paris, France. The Mona Lisa is perhaps the most famous painting in the world.

Pablo Escobar (1949-1993): infamous Colombian drug lord, narco-traficker, and head of a cocaine cartel. It was alleged that Escobar was killed in a shootout with US Special Forces, US intelligence, and the Colombian army (see Mark Bowden 2001. *Killing Pablo: the Hunt for the World's Greatest Outlaw*. New York: Penguin Books). Botero depicted Escobar in the infamous shootout leading to Escobar's death.

Guernica (1937): one of the most famous paintings of Pablo Picasso (1881-1973). It is an enormous political and anti-war mural made by Picasso in protest against the Franco Régime in Spain (1939-1975). This unique black-and-white "cubist" piece is now housed at the Museo Nacional Centro de Arte Reina Sofia in Madrid, Spain. *Guernica* depicts the Basque town of Guernica (Gernika) in Bizkaia, Spain, at the time when it was bombed on 26 April 1937 by the German Luftwaffe during the Spanish Civil War (1936-1939). There were as many as 400 deaths—mostly women and children as the townsmen were away fighting—a deliberate war atrocity allowed by Franco in collaboration with the German Nazis. The bombing lasted for more than two hours. (See: https://en.wikipedia.org/wiki/Guernica_(Picasso) and https://en.wikipedia.org/wiki/Bombing_of_Guernica) and also, Gernika Peace Museum Foundation, Gernikako Bakearen Museoa Fundazioa, Fundación Museo de la Paz de Gernika: https://www.museodelapaz.org/index.php.)

Wounded Knee: The Wounded Knee Massacre took place on 29 December 1890, when the US military killed as many as 300 Lakota Native Americans, mostly women and children and old men, on the Pine Ridge Reservation of South Dakota, United States. (About 30 US Cavalry soldiers were lost in the massacre.) It is considered to be the worst mass-shooting in US history. Wounded Knee was also the last major confrontation between the US military and Native Americans. (See: https://en.wikipedia.org/wiki/Wounded_Knee_Massacre and see: Dee Brown 1970. *Bury My Heart at Wounded Knee: an Indian History of the American West*. New York: Holt, Rinehart, & Winston.)

Hobbesian: adjective deriving from the surname of Thomas Hobbes (1588-1679), an English philosopher, best known for the work, *Leviathan* (1651). Hobbes is often cited from his work *De Cive (On the Citizen)* (1642), and the Latin phrase, *bellum omnium contra omnes* or "war of all against all" is repeated in *Leviathan*.

Machiavellian: adjective deriving from the surname of Niccolò Machiavelli (1469-1527), an Italian-Florentine diplomat, philosopher, writer, and playwright, most famous for his work, *Il Principe (The Prince)*, 1513. The term "machiavellian" is applied to the cunning, scheming, and unscrupulous behaviour which he describes, based on his observations as to what succeeds in realpolitik.

Yemen
This poem is based upon a famous photo of a starving Yemeni girl, Amal Hussain, seven years old, taken in 2018 by *New York Times* photographer and journalist, Tyler Hicks. Amal died soon after the photo was taken and she became a symbol of the atrocities of the Yemeni civil war. This poem is dedicated to all those who have suffered from the civil war in Yemen (2015 up to the time of writing). The main combatants are the rebel (Shia) Houthis who control half the country against the Yemeni Hadi (Sunni) government who control most of the other half, and Al-Qaeda on the Peninsula who intercede. Siding with these different combatants in this ongoing civil war are Great Britain, the United States, France, Saudi Arabia, and Iran. Military aid to different sides in the civil war has

exacerbated the conflict. Having relatively little agriculture of its own, Yemen is heavily reliant on imported food but civil war actions have led to severe shortages, with resulting mass-starvation among the Yemeni population. (See: https://www.nytimes.com/2018/12/07/podcasts/the-daily/yemen-saudi-arabia-amal-hussain-photo.html and my own Op-Ed article in *PeaceVoice*, "Why Are We Allowing Yemen to Starve?" (November 21, 2018): http://www.peacevoice.info/2018/11/21/why-are-we-allowing-yemen-to-starve/.)

PART VII: FACTICIUS
Profugo
Profugo (Latin): "Homeless".

PART VIII: MACTANS
Trayvon
Trayvon Martin (1995-2012): African-American teenager fatally shot by a neighbourhood-watch coordinator, George Zimmerman, on the night of 26 February 2012 in Sanford, Florida. Seventeen-year old Trayvon was unarmed, while Zimmerman was armed. In the ensuing 2013 jury trial, Zimmerman was acquitted on the second-degree murder charges against him. Because of Zimmerman's acquittal, the "Black Lives Matter (BLM) Movement" began in the United States in 2013. It was initiated with the hashtag #BlackLivesMatter on social media and became nationally recognized following mass-protests following the questionable deaths of two further African-Americans, Michael Brown of Ferguson, Missouri, and Eric Garner of New York City.
(See: https://en.wikipedia.org/wiki/Shooting_of_Trayvon_Martin and https://en.wikipedia.org/wiki/Black_Lives_Matter and https://blacklivesmatter.com/news/.)

The President: the President of the United States at the time of the Trayvon Martin killing was Barak Obama. President Obama made the following statement to the media on 19 July 2013, "You know, when Trayvon Martin was first shot I said that this could have been my son. Another way of saying that is Trayvon Martin could have been me 35 years ago. And when you think about why, in the African American community at least, there's a lot of pain around what happened here, I think it's important to recognize that the African American community is looking at this issue through a set of experiences and a history that doesn't go away…"
(See The White House Press Archive: https://obamawhitehouse.archives.gov/the-press-office/2013/07/19/remarks-president-trayvon-martin.)

Orphean serenade: In Greek mythology, the singing and lyre-playing of Orpheus could enchant wild beasts. Because of his musical talents he was able to gain the conditional release from the Underworld of his dead wife, Eurydice. Unfortunately, he lost her again because, contrary to the agreed conditions, he gazed back at her when leaving Hades.

Carlos Santana (1947-): Mexican-American musician and guitar virtuoso, considered one of the greatest guitarists of all time.

B. B. King (1925-2015): considered one of the greatest blues musicians of all time. His playing of the electric guitar has had a profound influence on subsequent artists. He was not only inducted into the "Rock and Roll Hall of Fame" but was nicknamed, "The King of the Blues".

Billie Holliday (1915-1959): African-American blues and jazz singer. Abused as a child, she had a tragic life, experiencing several abusive relationships as an adult, and suffering alcohol and drug addictions. Her song, "Strange Fruit" (1939), about the lynching of African-Americans in the Southern United States, was perhaps her greatest hit.

"Lightening-Long John": old chain-gang song sung by African-Americans. There is evidence of it being sung in 1934 at Darrington State Prison Farm in Sandy Point, Texas, United States (See: http://historymatters.gmu.edu/d/5758/ .)

'Dry September': short story by William Faulkner (1897-1962). First published in 1931 in Scribner's Magazine, it tells the story of a forming and growing white lynch-mob in the South on a hot September evening. The white mob is intent on killing an African-American man who supposedly had insulted a white woman. Faulkner (from Mississippi) was awarded the Nobel Prize for Literature in 1949.

"Amazing Grace": a Christian hymn, first published in 1779. It was written by the English clergyman and former slaver, John Newton (1725-1807). It became a popular song because of its themes of forgiveness and redemption. (See: https://en.wikipedia.org/wiki/Amazing_Grace.)

I Know Why the Caged Bird Sings (1969): autobiography of the African-American poet, writer, and civil rights activist, Maya Angelou (1928-2014). In her lifetime, she received over 50 honorary degrees and numerous awards, including the Presidential Medal of Freedom in 2011.

Cornel West (1953-): well-regarded African-American academic and public intellectual. One of his best works is perhaps Race Matters (1993)

Boston: Beacon Press. In this book, he discusses the significance of race, leadership in the Black-American community, and the legacy of Malcolm X—he asks, how much does race matter in the American present?

"We are climbing Jacob's Ladder": an African-American spiritual slave song, perhaps originating as early as 1750.
(See: https://en.wikipedia.org/wiki/We_Are_Climbing_Jacob%27s_Ladder and a version of it being sung:
https://www.youtube.com/watch?v=7-qQsW6pdVM.)

Mr Brown
This poem is based upon the fate of the African-American teenager, Michael Brown (1996-2014), who was shot and killed in Ferguson, Missouri, a suburb of St. Louis, USA, on August 9, 2014 by a white police officer. Brown—only 18 years old at the time of his death—was shot at least six times. Brown's demise caused much civil unrest in Ferguson and much agitation elsewhere. Protesters believed Brown raised his hands in the air and yelled out, "don't shoot!", prior to being shot. This then became a protest slogan: "hands up, don't shoot"—however, it is questionable Michael Brown ever said this based upon eyewitness accounts. The white police officer, Darren Wilson, who fired the shot(s) that killed Brown, was later acquitted by a grand jury. In response to the shooting, President Obama vowed to set aside $75 million in funds for law enforcement to invest in body-cameras. There was also a negative backlash against police officers. Two NYPD officers were killed in Brooklyn and their suspected killer posted online that this was in response to the recent killings of African-Americans by police. Another reaction to the Brown killing was the beginning of the #BlackLivesMatter movement as noted earlier.
(See: https://en.wikipedia.org/wiki/Shooting_of_Michael_Brown and https://blacklivesmatter.com/never-forget-mike-brown/.)

This poem refers to and/or quotes from many sources, including songs, speeches, an interview. The details are below.

Marvin Gaye (1939-1984): popular African-American singer, songwriter, and record-producer. His song, "What's Going On" (1971), is a protest song of the era and was influenced by a police brutality incident and conversations with his brother about the Vietnam War (1955-1975).

Brother Frederick: Frederick Douglass (1818-1895), African-American abolitionist. In an 1857 speech, titled, "West India Emancipation", given in Canandaigua, New York, he declared in part, "If there is no struggle, there is no progress. Those who profess to favor freedom and yet deprecate agitation are men who want crops without plowing up the ground; they want rain without thunder and lightning. They want the ocean without the awful roar of its many waters." (See: https://www.blackpast.org/african-american-history/1857-frederick-douglass-if-there-no-struggle-there-no-progress/.)

Brother Malcolm: Malcolm X (1925-1965), American civil rights activist and Muslim minister.

"I am for truth ... I am for justice ... no matter who it is for ...no matter who tells it..." These lines in the poem break up a quotation from Malcolm X, said in an interview, "I am for truth, I am for justice, no matter who it is for, no matter who tells it..."

Muddy Waters (1913-1983): famous American blues singer and songwriter, nicknamed the "Father of Chicago Blues".

"Mannish Boy": song by Muddy Waters, first released in 1955. The song is an assertion of "Black manhood" and therefore contradicts the term, "boy", used in the American South when addressing or referring to an African-American man.
(See: https://en.wikipedia.org/wiki/Mannish_Boy.)

"Blind Willie Johnson" (1897-1945): American gospel-blues singer, preacher, and virtuoso guitarist, known for his slide guitar playing. It is thought Johnson was blinded by his stepmother. His song, "Jesus Make Up My Dyin Bed", was released in 1928.

"Brother Martin": Dr. Martin Luther King, Jr. (1929-1968), renowned African-American civil rights activist, Baptist preacher, peace activist, and practitioner of non-violence. After being one of the main leaders of the African-American Civil Rights Movement in the 1960s, after his, "I Have a Dream", speech, his March on Washington in 1963, and numerous other peaceful protest marches, and after being awarded the Nobel Prize for Peace in 1964, King was assassinated in Memphis, Tennessee in 1968, allegedly by James Earl Ray.

"Darkness cannot drive out darkness": In a version of his speech, "Loving Your Enemies" (given on several occasions), Dr Martin Luther King was quoted (in December 1957) as saying the words, "Darkness cannot drive out darkness, only light can do that..."
(See: http://ipoet.com/ARCHIVE/BEYOND/King-Jr/Loving-Your-Enemies.html.)

"The Sky is Crying": song by Gary B. B. Coleman (1947-1994) highly regarded by many blues aficionados.

Gary B. B. Coleman (1947-1994): a famous soul-blues singer, songwriter, and record producer from Texas.

"The time is always ripe to do right...": Dr. Martin Luther King, Jr., "Remaining Awake Through a Great Revolution", 1968, sermon (his last) given at the National Cathedral in Washington, D.C. A fuller quotation from King's sermon would be, "One is the myth of time. It is the notion that only time can solve the problem of racial injustice... Somewhere we must come to see that human progress never rolls in on the wheels of inevitability. It comes through the tireless efforts and the persistent work of dedicated individuals who are willing to be co-workers with God. And without this hard work, time itself becomes an ally of the primitive forces of social stagnation. So we must help time and realize that the time is always ripe to do right."
(See: https://kinginstitute.stanford.edu/king-papers/publications/knock-midnight-inspiration-great-sermons-reverend-martin-luther-king-jr-10.)

Ferguson and Dred Scott: The Dred Scott v Sandford US Supreme Court Case (1857) is again cited here. Dred Scott sought his freedom while living in Missouri, a slave state, even though Scott had lived most of his life a free man in the territories of present-day Minnesota and Michigan. The Michael Brown shooting took place in Ferguson, Missouri. It seems that, again, the racist history of the US was repeating itself in the same state but for different reasons. (See note above for more about the Dred Scott US Supreme Court decision.)

Compromise in 1820: The Missouri Compromise of 1820 is referenced because again the Michael Brown shooting took place in Missouri. Thus, in my view, Missouri, as a place, has been a potent symbol of racial controversy in the racist history of the United States. Missouri in essence became a litmus test of compromise between those upholding slavery and those wishing to abolish that institution and not only through the Dred Scott case (1857) but earlier with the Compromise of 1820. Therefore, the Compromise of 1820, or the Missouri Compromise of 1820, stipulated that if Missouri were to be admitted in the union of the United States as a "slave state" then Maine would have to be admitted the same year as a "free state", thereby maintaining the balance between slave and free states at the time. It must be remembered too that the United States Constitution stipulated each state shall have two US Senators whereas the US House of Representatives shall be a representative legislative body based upon population. In this manner, small states would have equal representation as

larger and more populous states in the US Senate. By 1820 in the United States, the slavery question between Northern and Southern states was very divisive. Both Northern and Southern states wished to keep an even balance between slave states and free states, so as to keep the "balance of power" between states in the US Senate whereby there would be an equal number of slave-holding states and of free states. So, if a new state were to be admitted as a slave state in the South then a new Northern state would have to be admitted as free (as was the case with Missouri (slave) and Maine (free)). Hence, by 1821, there were 12 slave-holding states and 12 free states in the union. What is more, the so-called historical "Compromise of 1820" went further. The Compromise of 1820 stipulated that above the 36° 30'parallel line any new territories becoming new states in the union must be admitted as "free states" and "not" as slave states. The 36° 30' parallel line is the Southern border of Missouri, so all new states above this line with the exception of Missouri had to be admitted as "free states". Any states below the 36° 30'parallel line could be admitted as "slave states". The territory above the 36° 30'parallel line was an enormous unorganized territory and a largely unpopulated (with the exception of Native peoples) wilderness at the time, the very same territory which was purchased from France by the third president, Thomas Jefferson, and known as the Louisiana Purchase (1803). Yet, by 1850, with the 1850 Compromise, the promise of the 1820 Compromise became null and void because some of these new territories and some newer territories acquired as a result of the Mexican-American War (1846-1848) were permitted to decide for themselves through popular voting how they should be admitted into the union, a democratic decision by the people, which became known as "Popular Sovereignty". So, in 1854, with the passage of the Kansas-Nebraska Act, the Missouri Compromise of 1820 became nullified as those north-western territories would decide for themselves whether or not to be free or slave.
(See: https://www.history.com/topics/abolitionist-movement/missouri-compromise
and https://en.m.wikipedia.org/wiki/Missouri_Compromise.)

Howlin' Wolf: Howlin' Wolf (Chester Arthur Burnett) (1910-1976), American blues singer, guitarist, harmonica player, one of the most well-known Chicago blues singers, originally from Mississippi.

The song "Poor Boy" was originally released in 1956 and sung by Elvis Presley (who wrote it along with Vera Matson). The first words of the song are, "I'm a poor boy". Howlin' Wolf also covered the song.

The song, "Boom Boom", was originally released in 1962 under the Vee-Jay Label. In many respects, "Boom Boom" became the signature song of Jonny Lee Hooker (see below).

"Johnny Lee Hooker" (1917-2001): American blues singer, songwriter, and virtuoso blues guitarist. He was a highly original blues artist, combining Delta Mississippi Blues with Northern Mississippi styles, and with an idiosyncratic use of the electric guitar. It has been asserted that he had his own "boogie" style of blues.
(See: https://en.wikipedia.org/wiki/John_Lee_Hooker.)

Parkland
The mass-shooting at Marjory Stoneman Douglas High School in Parkland, Broward County, Florida occurred on 14 February 2018 (Saint Valentine's Day). On that day, seventeen people were killed and seventeen more were injured. The perpetrator was nineteen-year old Nikolas Cruz, an expelled student from the school. It was the deadliest mass high school shooting in the United States. Tragically, a year after the incident, two student survivors committed suicide. Also, the Broward County Sheriff was criticized for allowing the shooter, who had mental health issues, to obtain a firearm following many reports of Cruz posting negative and threatening messages on social-media sites. The Broward Sheriff was further criticized for not responding to the scene more quickly and confronting the shooter. Following this mass-shooting, there was a concerted effort to push for gun-control legislation but to date no substantial legislation has been passed by the US Congress. Moreover, some of the wrongful conspiracy theories following the mass-shooting falsely accused various Stoneman Douglas High School students as being "crisis actors".
(See:
https://en.wikipedia.org/wiki/Stoneman_Douglas_High_School_shooting.)
Unfortunately, mass-school shootings like the one at Stoneman Douglas High School have become more and more frequent since the Columbine High School shooting in Colorado in 1999.

The high school is named after the writer, journalist, and environmental activist, Marjory Stoneman Douglas (1890-1998) who wrote the well-regarded book: *Everglades: River of Grass* (1947; new edn. 1997). Sarasota, FL: Pineapple Press.)

"Ashes! Ashes! We all fall down": The American version of the nursery rhyme goes:

> Ring-a-round the rosie,
> A pocket full of posies,
> Ashes! Ashes!
> We all fall down.

Some scholars have conjectured that the rhyme refers to the Bubonic Plague of Europe, or the Great Plague in England in 1665. But this is mostly folkloric speculation. There is no concrete evidence to support such claims about this nursery rhyme and its origins. Other scholars have asserted that the rhymes originally had to do with "pagan rites". Even so, various European countries have different variations of the rhyme. (See: https://en.wikipedia.org/wiki/Ring_a_Ring_o%27_Roses#cite_ref-Delamar2001pp38-9_4-1 and https://www.snopes.com/fact-check/ring-around-rosie/.)

Pa-hay-Okee: Seminole Indian word meaning "grassy waters", a descriptor for the Everglades.

Al-la-pat-tah: Seminole Indian word, meaning, "alligator".

Wee-lus-tee: Seminole Indian word, meaning, "black-water". (See: http://www.yallaha.com/documents/Seminole%20Dictionary.pdf.)

A day for young love: The day of the shooting was Valentine's Day, 14 February 2018.

Jack-in-the-Box: a toy, outwardly a box with a crank. When the crank is turned a tune plays and normally at the end of the melody, but sometimes at random, a clown or jester pops out of the box. Many Jack-in-the-Box toys play the nursery rhyme, "Pop Goes the Weasel". (See: https://en.wikipedia.org/wiki/Jack-in-the-box and https://en.wikipedia.org/wiki/Pop_Goes_the_Weasel.)

Crosses, stars of David, mala beads, crescent moons: symbols for Christianity, Judaism, Buddhism, and Islam, the four major world religions. While the majority of the victims were Christian and five of those killed were Jewish, it is unclear if any were Buddhist or Muslim. However, as a poet, I am using artistic license here to include all of the world's major religions to symbolize that such tragedies affect all of us regardless of religious affiliation and religious beliefs.

AR-15 (ArmaLite Rifle Model 15): a type of automatic and assault weapon. In 1959, Colt arms manufacturing company acquired rights to the weapon, and then began making its own version. The shooter, Nikolas Cruz, used this style of weapon in the Marjory Stoneman Douglas High School mass-shooting in 2018 as did shooters in many of the other mass-shootings in recent years, such as the one at Sandy Hook Elementary School in Connecticut in 2012, the San Bernardino attack in 2015, and the Las Vegas shooting in 2017. In recent years, such assault weapons, with the capability of shooting multiple rounds in seconds and the potential for mass loss of life, have been questioned in terms of the necessity for allowing them in the hands of the public. Many have urged the US Congress to ban such assault-weapons as the AR-15 style rifles but as of the time of writing nothing has been done.

J.P. LINSTSROTH'S *EPOCHAL RECKONINGS*
ADVANCE COMMENTS

Linstroth's angry panorama of the late 20th and early 21st centuries will be familiar from media reports and is written in appropriate verse, prose and diction. Scenes of displacement, attempts to survive nature's violence, those seeking refuge, social and racial discrimination are attributed to civil war, capitalism, globalisation, fear and hatred of others as well as President Trump's evil destruction of American idealism. This is an anti-epic mapping our time.

—**Bruce King,** author / editor of *The Internationalization of English Literature, The New English Literatures, New National and Post-colonial Literatures*, etc.

With the finesse and erudition of a classicist, and yet the clarion urgency of a contemporary activist, J.P. Linstroth ably chronicles the struggles of those whose tales are both sung and unsung. While his lyrical invocations speak of historical and contemporary oppression, the varied sufferings of marginalised peoples and more widespread catastrophes around the globe, he infuses his verse with cultural richness, resilience and human indomitability.

—**Akin Jeje**, author of *Smoked Pearl: Poems of Hong Kong and Beyond*, Proverse 2010.

To reckon is to count. Words count, as the body-bags have counted up throughout the twenty-first century. The attempt in this volume of poetry recording modern catastrophe after modern catastrophe, some of them echoing ancient catastrophes, is to reckon with what has been disastrous, and with what becomes mere anonymous numbers. Linstroth's poetry believes in the value of words, and of people within different countries; he attempts not to let us forget them either.

— **Jeremy Tambling**, Professor of English at SWAP University Warsaw; and before retiring, Professor of Comparative Literature in Hong Kong, and Professor of Literature at Manchester

SOME POETRY AND POETRY COLLECTIONS
Published by Proverse Hong Kong

Alphabet, by Andrew S. Guthrie. 2015.

Astra and Sebastian, by L.W. Illsley. 2011.

Bliss of Bewilderment, by Birgit Bunzel Linder. 2017.

The Burning Lake, by Jonathan Locke Hart. 2016.

Celestial Promise, by Hayley Ann Solomon. 2017.

Chasing light, by Patricia Glinton Meicholas. 2013.

China suite and other poems,
by Gillian Bickley. 2009.

Epochal Reckonings, by J.P. Linstroth, 2020. *(Scheduled.)*

For the record and other poems of Hong Kong,
by Gillian Bickley. 2003.

Frida Kahlo's cry and other poems,
by Laura Solomon. 2015.

Grandfather's Robin, by Gillian Bickley, 2020. *(Scheduled)*

Heart to Heart: Poems, by Patty Ho. 2010.

Home, away, elsewhere,
by Vaughan Rapatahana. 2011.

Hong Kong Growing Pains, by Jon Ng. 2020. *(Scheduled)*

Immortelle and bhandaaraa poems,
by Lelawattee Manoo-Rahming. 2011.

In vitro, by Laura Solomon. 2nd ed. 2014.

Irreverent poems for pretentious people,
by Henrik Hoeg. 2016.

The layers between (essays and poems),
by Celia Claase. 2015.

Of leaves & ashes, by Patty Ho. 2016.

Life Lines, by Shahilla Shariff. 2011.

Mingled voices: the international Proverse Poetry Prize anthology 2016, edited by Gillian and Verner Bickley. 2017.

Mingled voices 2: the international Proverse Poetry Prize anthology 2017, edited by Gillian and Verner Bickley. 2018.

Mingled voices 3: the international Proverse Poetry Prize anthology 2018, edited by Gillian and Verner Bickley. 2019.

Mingled voices 4: the international Proverse Poetry Prize anthology 2019, edited by Gillian and Verner Bickley. 2020.

Moving house and other poems from Hong Kong,
by Gillian Bickley. 2005.

Over the Years: Selected Collected Poems, 1972-2015,
by Gillian Bickley. 2017.

Painting the borrowed house: poems,
by Kate Rogers. 2008.

Perceptions, by Gillian Bickley. 2012.

Poems from the Wilderness,
by Jack Mayer, 2020. (*Scheduled.*)

Rain on the pacific coast,
by Elbert Siu Ping Lee. 2013.

refrain, by Jason S. Polley. 2010.

Savage Charm, by Ahmed Elbeshlawy. 2019.

Shadow play, by James Norcliffe. 2012.

Shadows in deferment, by Birgit Bunzel Linder. 2013.

Shifting sands, by Deepa Vanjani. 2016.

Sightings: a collection of poetry, with an essay, 'communicating poems', by Gillian Bickley. 2007.

Smoked pearl: poems of Hong Kong and beyond, by Akin Jeje (Akinsola Olufemi Jeje). 2010.

Of symbols misused, by Mary-Jane Newton. 2011.

The Hummingbird Sometimes Flies Backwards, by D.J. Hamilton. 2019.

The Year of the Apparitions, by José Manuel Sevilla. 2020.

Unlocking, by Mary-Jane Newton. March 2014.

Violet, by Carolina Ilica. March 2019.

Wonder, lust & itchy feet, by Sally Dellow. 2011.

FIND OUT MORE ABOUT PROVERSE AUTHORS, BOOKS, EVENTS AND LITERARY PRIZES

Visit our website: http://www.proversepublishing.com
Visit our distributor's website: www.cup.cuhk.edu.hk
Follow us on Twitter
Follow news and conversation: twitter.com/Proversebooks
OR
Copy and paste the following to your browser window and follow
the instructions: https://twitter.com/#!/ProverseBooks
"Like" us on www.facebook.com/ProversePress

Request our free E-Newsletter
Send your request to info@proversepublishing.com.

Availability
Available in Hong Kong and world-wide from our Hong Kong
based distributor, The Chinese University of Hong Kong Press, The
Chinese University of Hong Kong,
Shatin, NT, Hong Kong SAR, China.
Email: cup@cuhk.edu.hk
Website: www.cup.cuhk.edu.hk.

All titles are available from Proverse Hong Kong,
http://www.proversepublishing.com

Most titles can be ordered online from amazon (various countries).

Stock-holding retailers
Hong Kong (CUHKP, Bookazine)
Canada (Elizabeth Campbell Books),
Andorra (Llibreria La Puça, La Llibreria).

Orders may be made from bookshops in the UK and elsewhere.

Ebooks
Most of our titles are available also as Ebooks.